Choose

Your

Super Power

Live with Purpose, On Purpose, and
Rock Your Super Self

D.C. Hackerott

Orange Cape Publishing
Riley, KS

Edited by Spencer Borup
Spencer.borup@gmail.com

Cover by Cizlini Arts
chroosthen@gmail.com

Formatted by Debbie Lum
debbie@debbiestevenlum.com

www.chooseyoursuperpower.com

ISBN: 978-0-9980762-1-8

This book is dedicated to my parents, who always believed in my potential, even when I was the shy kid trying to hide from the world. Their love and belief in me allowed me to embark on my own journey toward finding my purpose.

Contents

Introduction

The Path of the Superhero

Superheroes rarely have a smooth path to becoming Super. In fact, most of them start out in pretty ordinary circumstances, undergo an amazing transformation—both internal and external—and come out with amazing Super Powers. And their transformation doesn't stop there. They still have internal challenges, relationship issues, all while saving the world. They are tested in super-big ways like only a Superhero can be tested.

It's the fact that they usually come from rather ordinary backgrounds like the rest of us that endears them to us initially. We continue to notice ourselves in them as they work through their struggles. We all have a hope of becoming Super. They give us hope that it's possible. Throughout *Choose Your Super Power*, we will delve into the process of how you too can undergo a massive transformation and develop your own Super Powers. And just like our favorite Superheroes . . . you will be tested.

Once you are aware of the choices you have in your life, the true tests begin. We are surrounded by choices each and every day—

big and small, seemingly important and apparently not. Once you know the truth, you will never be able to view your choices the same way again. The compounding effects of your choices will magnify your power, your passion, and your purpose.

Has anyone ever asked you what your Super Power would be if you could have just one? I've enjoyed asking this question for years. The answer can be quite telling and provide a window into their world. You learn how they really feel about themselves and the world they live in. Do they feel in control? Or do they feel like a victim? Do they look for escape, adrenaline, or simply to be in a more powerful place? Answer that now for yourself: If you could choose only one Super Power, what would it be? Why? Tell me about the feelings it gives you to know that you have the power, and also how you feel when you *use* your Super Power.

The options are endless: flying, super-speed, teleportation, mind-reading, super-strength, invincibility, invisibility, X-ray vision, laser vision, bullet-proof, healing touch, and so many more.

Did you choose the ability to fly? Close your eyes and imagine yourself soaring over houses and through the clouds. How about super strength? Imagine that your incredible strength allows you to pick up and move anything you want at any point—how exciting it would be to feel those muscles grow taut as you flex. Or wouldn't it be nice to be fast? Pretend you are running at supersonic speed and able to be anywhere in the world within minutes if you choose; the wind rushes past as you dodge around raindrops, never being touched. What if your touch could heal people, cure cancer, lift it from their bodies and restore people to perfect health? How would that make you feel?

It really is possible to feel this way. When you choose *your* Super Power, it will feel just right. You will be in your element and feel invincible. Your Super Power will be *yours*. It's a perfect fit, like wearing a glove that fits with precision. There will be no other speedsters, strongmen, or aliens who can fly and shoot lasers out of their eyes quite like you. It will be yours. All yours.

Will there be tradeoffs and challenges? Of course! You won't be able to do everything or save everyone. People will question you, challenge you in ways you never knew possible. You will challenge yourself, and by doing so be able to accomplish far more than you ever thought possible. On the other side of every challenge is your chance, your choice, to come out stronger than you were before.

The three components we will explore are Autonomy, Purpose, and Mastery, as well as their interaction with one another. They will weave together to make the fabric of your life moving forward, a life with purpose and a purpose you choose. You will wake each day excited for what that day will bring and lay your head on the pillow at night knowing that you gave all you had.

During each day, you will be given a litmus test by which you can gauge your decisions, your actions, and your mental preparedness for what might come next. You will tackle challenges and find opportunities in them. People you have known much of your life will ask you what has changed. They may barely recognize the new you. The face is the same, but there's something . . . different. It's your drive, your determination, your passion and purpose for life.

In the past, you may have had a taste of this, but it was fleeting. You yearn to have it back, to be aflame with that passion again. Or perhaps you have never before had that feeling of being truly alive and invigorated, and still yearn for what you've seen and heard from others.

Either way, the choice is yours. You will learn how to discover it, design it, and deploy it. Then you will be in a constant cycle of rediscovery, redesign, and redeployment as you reach even greater heights. This, my friends, is an adventure. This is more than just designing your life; it's designing your purpose to achieve the most fulfilling life. Shall we begin the adventure that will be your life?

Overview of the Sections and Order of Attack: From Today Through Mastery

In order to have a clear path to developing your Super Power, we will walk together through the three stages of development. We will discuss the potential threats that may come your way and how to tackle those. We will see how important it is to overcome "average" and what others do to kill their dreams and goals, then set out on a mission to dominate yours. The order of attack for these three sections is critical. Don't skip around. Read them in order and witness the benefits of the building process and the compounding effect.

1. **Autonomy:** We start by developing *autonomy*. Every Superhero must undergo the journey of determining where they are in relation to others and work toward being independent. They must find autonomy. The Merriam-Webster Dictionary defines autonomy as, "1: the quality or state of being self-governing; 2: self-directing freedom and especially moral independence."

   - Your state of being is your choice. It is not something given or granted by other people. If you want it, you must choose it wisely and carefully.

   - Self-governing and self-directing freedom are choices that are up to you to make, and no one else. Once you have autonomy, you have absolute responsibility for both the choices you make and the consequences that come from those choices. If you make a mistake, it is up to you to fix it. You can never again be the "victim" and expect others to come to your rescue.

   - Moral independence and values should be aligned with the choices you make to keep you in a state of self-directed freedom. Purpose is interwoven with your values and ensures the best chances of success in remaining morally independent.

   - Moral independence cannot be had when following the norms of others and their broken or faulty moral compasses. Moral independence infers that your moral code is separated from the rationalizations made by average people; you hold yourself to a more consistent (and often higher) moral code of ethics.

2. **Purpose:** According to a site developed to help churches determine their *purpose*, I found a fitting description, for our needs, of a purpose statement. "A purpose statement captures succinctly *why the organization exists and what it does*. It should be *memorable* enough so that everyone connected to the organization can *remember it and use it*. . . . A solid purpose statement . . . can be easily used as a *benchmark for decision-making and planning*."

   - It *captures* (I love the visual this creates) why you exist and what you do. Your purpose is your choice; it defines you. You capture it and make it your own. This is where you begin aligning with your moral compass.

   - Purpose is memorable enough that you can easily remember it and use it. It should be woven intentionally into the fabric of your daily life and decision-making as well as your long-term planning.

   - Your purpose is a benchmark for your decision-making and planning. Your purpose serves as a litmus test to help determine what you do, how you do it, and when it is achieved. If it doesn't fit your purpose, it doesn't fit your life. A litmus test, in this context, is a way to verify that you are pursuing the right path.

3. **Mastery:** Synonyms for *mastery* include words like "command" and "dominion," typically over a subject or area. I love the emotions that these evoke. They feel right for a Super Power and for a Superhero. Have *command* over yourself and your skills and abilities in order to have *dominion* over your "kingdom," world, and purpose.

   - Think of *dominion* as your "kingdom." Do you rule your dominion or does it rule you? Can you control your actions? It's hard to encourage others to take action when you procrastinate. Do you frequently oversleep, and are you late to everything? Or do you honor your commitments to yourself and others? You have to develop mastery of yourself first. If you cannot control yourself, how can you expect to have dominion over your "kingdom" (i.e. purpose)?

   - Constant incremental improvement is the choice that continues to strengthen your Super Power and yield additional compounding effects.

   - As we move through Mastery, we will outline several key Mindsets which are valuable additions to your toolbox. A glossary of these is at the end of the book for reference.

Once you have Autonomy, Purpose, and Mastery, you have your Super Power and the ability to use it effectively. Let's get started!

PART 1

Autonomy

Superheroes don't often start out as either super or heroic. Even though they are generally good, well-meaning people, they usually haven't done very much that would qualify as heroic. Most "Supers" don't even have direction or confidence in their lives yet. It is a growing process—much like that of a butterfly emerging from its cocoon. But for those who will become Supers, change is coming. It always does. What's coming for you? I'll give you one guess.

1. Change is Coming

Change is coming. Either by crisis or by choice. You choose which. We all do. Change is inevitable. Everything in our lives is constantly changing. Even if you have a very predictable routine that you follow methodically every day, the truth is that everything is changing, if not drastically then at least subtly.

Every day you wake to a long-established routine of the same exercises, followed by meditation and prayer, after which you shower and have a cup of coffee while you fix your hair. It changes over time, though. Your hair is longer, shorter, grayer. The exercises become a little more challenging as you get older, or a little less challenging as your fitness improves. The coffee is a little sweeter, waking up harder, if you didn't go to bed at quite the same time. Our bodies and minds are designed for change. In fact, we crave it. When we have no change, we get bored. We seek change, something to break the tedium of schedule.

So why do so many people say that they hate change? The answer is obvious: If the change is not their choice, they won't embrace it easily. It's out of their control, and people want control just as much as they want change. Because of this desire for constant control, there are many people out there— maybe even you—who fight against any change. They complain endlessly about changes at work, getting older, the kids growing up, everything. Let's take a few minutes to break this down to see why some people are so opposed to change.

There are generally two types of change. One type is short-lived. It's the diet or exercise routine that we will do long enough to see some results before we regress to our old eating or exercise habits. It is studying for your classes until the semester is over and you can take a "much deserved break." You never really intend to make it permanent because that would be too hard and deny yourself something you want. It is something you merely attempt to survive, to push through for a short period of time.

Most people can't imagine living with the short-lived change for the rest of their lives. It's overwhelming, scary, and downright depressing. This is why people don't like change (at least in this form). It's painful. It's even more painful when you feel external pressure to change.

The other type of change is a full transformation. With transformation, your motives are different. You may want this change desperately or you may literally have no choice but to make it permanent. You have been diagnosed with diabetes and either drastically change your eating and fitness habits or you die. You just witnessed a friend dying of lung cancer and can't fathom going through that unimaginable pain yourself and not seeing your children or grandchildren graduate from high school, so you quit smoking.

For others, it's an epiphany—lightning strikes their brain in a rush of deep understanding—and their view of their world has completely changed. Perhaps there is some other tragedy, either minor or major, that has hit your life in such a profound way that you cannot imagine your life without a fundamental transformation in some area. Having children will do that to some people.

Regardless of what drives it, this type of change is fundamentally different. You have a powerful and compelling WHY. It drives you. You don't need to drive it. The change *will* happen. The only question is what and who you will be when it's complete.

Butterflies and Moths:
What Does Transformation Look Like?

Have you ever watched a child as they hit a growth spurt? It's fascinating. They eat everything in sight. They often spend a few weeks getting somewhat chubby. Soon after, they sleep constantly and barely eat at all. What on earth is happening? They're growing. Their bodies crave food and energy because they need it for their little bodies to grow. They sleep constantly and barely eat when the actual growth is happening.

Much like the growing child, a caterpillar eats nonstop until it too builds its cocoon, crawls inside to hibernate, and emerges as a beautiful butterfly . . . or a moth. More on the moth later. This fat, slow, plodding, often so-ugly-it's-cute creature comes out completely transformed and able to fly! Wow! Do you understand how incredible that is? Just think about the amazing work that has to happen in that tiny space of the cocoon to form this complex and beautiful creature, completely transformed.

Like both the growing child and the transforming caterpillar, you are in the midst of a change, a growing experience. If you are anything like me, you gorge yourself on personal development in many forms—podcasts, books, coaching, seminars, and workshops. Even though most experts recommend focusing on only one change at a time, I find myself needing to enter as much information as I can into my mind—good ideas, good "fuels," tips and tricks, habits, and more. Then I let my brain disseminate the information. I let it ferment.

Almost six years ago, I did this at work. I went through an exhaustive national search of best business practices of those who are highly successful and don't follow the normal "recipe." I knew that there had to be better, more efficient ways to be of far greater service to our clients. And guess what? I was right.

After I had collected all of the information that I could find, I thought about it at length. I went for long walks and let my mind wander as I went into something that resembled a mental cocoon. What emerged was a fantastic, new, innovative system that we now share with both our clients and others in our firm. I came out a butterfly.

Please don't misunderstand, it wasn't merely *thinking* that created the new ideas. It was letting go of the intense thought, and, once the idea came, acting on it. More on that later.

You can do this too. When you gather the information, even if you don't necessarily know where it will lead, you are feeding your mind. Choose wisely what you feed it. Be intentional about what enters your mind. Attend trainings and conferences through work and on your own. Look forward to these. You can gain something from every situation, if you only *look*.

Look for the nuggets of knowledge. With eyes wide open, you'll find them everywhere. Choose to open your eyes to see them. As you feed your mind, you will start to have a clear focus about your direction and your purpose.

Remember also that the little caterpillar doesn't just take naps in that little cocoon or sit there thinking of what a beautiful butterfly it could become. There is action. You need to take action, too. We will discuss action and having an Experimenter's Mindset more in-depth in a later section.

When you come out of your cocoon, will you be the butterfly or the moth? Forgive me if you are a moth lover. Unlike a moth, a butterfly can captivate us. You don't see children chasing moths or grown men taking pictures of them to show their little daughters. Butterflies hold a special place for many of us. They are beauty in flight, grace in motion. What determines whether you reenter the world as a butterfly or a moth? Simple.

People follow butterflies. People try to get rid of moths. Do people follow you or flee from you? Are you leading with your purpose, in service to others? Or is your purpose merely about furthering your own existence? If your purpose is primarily self-centered, people will treat you like a moth. They won't want you in the house because you'll ruin their things (like too many of my sweaters). They'll try their best to keep you away from the things they value.

Butterflies are loved and admired by children and adults both. When someone sees a butterfly, they really want it to linger as long as possible. They don't try to get rid of it. In the end, butterflies bring joy and vitality. Do you?

This transformation that you will undergo as we continue down this path of designing, developing, and deploying your Super Power will lead you to either attracting or repelling people. To understand the fundamentals of how to develop your Super Power, your Super Purpose, we need to take a look at what's really going on out there in the world. What choices are people making? What has gone wrong that requires the need of our Super Powers, and how can we combat the impacts these wrong choices have on ourselves?

To develop autonomy, that self-governance required of us, we need to develop an awareness of the power of choice.

2. The Power of Choice

The Daily Choice

You have a choice every day when you wake up. We all do. It's the same choice for everyone, regardless of where you are in life. You wake up every day with the choice to view your day, your life, your world as a series of OBSTACLES or a series of OPPORTUNITIES.

The OBSTACLE Mindset

Most people wake up each day and choose to view people, events, and life in general as a series of OBSTACLES. Please understand, these are not bad people. They simply choose to react in negative ways. They are often considered part of the "herd" as they follow one bad news story after another. Some even think the world is out to get them. Most, however, just focus on the obstacle instead of looking a little past the herd to see the opportunity that waits on the other side.

It doesn't take much looking to find these folks. They surround us. The stock market goes down and they bail out, assuming that it will drop to zero (which it never has). There's a chicken pox outbreak nearby and they assume that they will be next to get it. Other airports have announced weather delaying flights, and they assume their flight will be cancelled and their vacation ruined. A long-time friend whom they have fallen out of touch with has cancer, and they are depressed that they haven't stayed in closer contact over the last few years.

Do you know people like this? Are you guilty of being one? We can all be this way from time to time. That's why the choice is a *daily* choice. No one is perfect. Some days, even those with an Obstacle Mindset are capable of finding opportunity.

The challenge is that most people fail to recognize that they even have a choice at all. They go with their initial reactions, natural tendencies, and follow the herd. It takes frequent practice to change your Obstacle Mindset to an Opportunity Mindset. It never ends. Setbacks happen. The key is to *choose* to build or to regain an OPPORTUNITY Mindset.

Change is one of those areas in which we have a choice. Is change an obstacle for you? Dig in deeply to figure out why you view change negatively. Is it because of something specific about what is changing? Is it because you didn't choose the change? Will it really negatively affect you personally? And, most importantly, how can you find your opportunity in the change?

The OPPORTUNITY Mindset

Have you ever met someone who seems to find opportunities everywhere? Maybe they get "stuck" in the long, slow line at the store only to come out the other side with stories of an amazing person they met in line. In fact, they tend to find friends everywhere. Everyone wants to be around them.

They are given opportunities to go backstage at concerts, are given free stuff all the time, and never seem to have a bad day, no matter what happens. I've known many in my life. The natural tendency is to attribute all of this to luck. But let's not be so quick in that attribution.

When you meet a positive, upbeat person, especially when you are in a challenging situation, aren't you attracted to them? Don't you want to be near them, befriend them, hang out with them? Isn't their optimism downright addictive? Infectious? That's how they get that "luck." They are willing to get out of the Obstacle Mindset and learn about people and find opportunities no matter the situation.

Most opportunities are found in interacting with others. Few opportunities are found while looking at a smartphone, tablet, or other screen. Opportunists find opportunity in the people they meet, and often in serving them in some way. Even something as simple as a smile and a kind word can change the direction of someone's day.

In today's technology era, we are losing our ability to have meaningful conversations with others. To be inspired and inspiring. But this is no obstacle for people with an

Opportunity Mindset—they have the uncanny ability to see beyond themselves and their current situations.

Do you spend most of your time with an obstacle or an Opportunity Mindset? Where are you in the herd? Even those who lead the herd can have an Obstacle Mindset. Imagine a herd of bison standing majestically on a beautiful plateau full of lush grass. Think about life as part of the herd.

Herd Mentality

When things are going well, the herd stands there eating grass, never considering to search for more or better-tasting grass. They take long, unencumbered naps. They look and act just like everyone else in the group. That's what being part of the herd means.

There *are* benefits to being in the herd. You are less exposed, on an individual basis, to external threats. You usually move together to find food and shelter—no need to go forage by yourself. You can usually sleep peacefully, knowing that the herd surrounds you.

Who wouldn't want to be part of a herd? Sounds like a pretty good life . . . unless someone in your herd gets a life-threatening, contagious disease. Then that disease can wipe out your entire herd. Worse yet, if a few in the herd get spooked, it becomes a stampede. What happens to a stampeding herd?

One member of the herd gets spooked by something, anything, and starts to run. With no idea why there is a panic, others in the herd start running away from the supposed "threat." They are in the flight mode of the fight-or-flight sequence and are often running blindly. The sick, old, and weak are often either trampled or left behind. Do you remember the tales from the Old West when large herds of buffalo would run over the side of a cliff?

People with an Obstacle Mindset are the herd. They thunder right over the proverbial cliff again and again. Even though they often know it's coming, they run blindly to their own demise. They *react* instead of *act*.

Consider the behaviors of many individual investors over the last 20 years. Even though overall markets (S&P 500) have averaged 9.9%, individual investors averaged 2.5% over the same time period. Why? Because they saw market volatility as an obstacle instead of an opportunity.

How many politicians use the thundering herd to sweep them into office? How many radio and television programs and ads are designed to spook you into being part of the herd? We are often ruled by fear and greed, both of which are obstacles.

Not all of us choose to be part of the herd. When the thundering herd has run over the edge of the cliff, the opportunists look around and admire how much grass is left there for them. Taking advantage of opportunities is how people create wealth over the long term.

Wealth is much more than money (or "grass"). It is the richness of a fulfilling life. It is waking up in the morning with a purpose that drives you to become an even better person today. It is having a keen eye for the opportunities missed by many others. Members of the herd will be upset with and resent those who take advantage of opportunities to create these kinds of wealth.

In my early years as a financial advisor, I thought it was my job to save people from making investment mistakes. I thought I needed to rescue the world, or at least my community. I soon realized that there are many people who really do want to run themselves over the side of the cliff and commit financial suicide by operating based on emotion. I exhausted myself trying to help them. Though a few listened and flourished through rough markets, some insisted on doing the opposite of what it took to come out ahead. They had an Obstacle Mindset.

My fellow opportunists, the ones I still work with today, have learned to take advantage of opportunities that arise. We are invigorated by our ability to grow in spite of, and partly because of, market volatility.

My lesson in all of this? If people do not want to be saved, no amount of effort can save them from their destructive ways. Focus instead on the people who are willing to adopt the Opportunity Mindset. I hope that's you!

Some people come hardwired to look for opportunities. Some do not. Most opportunists come to it through experience—the hard way. I once heard that *experience* is learning from your own mistakes; *wisdom* is learning from the mistakes of others. If you come to your Opportunity Mindset through *experience*, you quickly learn the value of *wisdom*! This is the true path to a Growth Mindset, which we will discuss in a future chapter.

Life and Death

Are you truly living? Or just waiting around to die? No matter how obvious the answer might seem—you are, after all, reading this book—I want you to take a moment and consider this. Benjamin Franklin was paraphrased by George S. Patton brilliantly when he said, "Most people die at a very early age, only to be buried forty or fifty years later."

In my daily life as a financial advisor and the co-owner of a martial arts facility, I talk to all types of people from all walks of life every day. I have a client at the office, Sue, who was so excited (and occasionally apprehensive) about retirement that she gave herself high blood pressure, heart palpitations, and panic attacks. She would call me on her cellphone from the parking lot at work to ask me the same question repeatedly, without listening to the answer. "Are you sure I'll be okay? *Really* sure? I need to get out of here. It's killing me. Are you sure I can retire? Please, say yes!"

About a year after her retirement (which made her immensely happy), she was back to her old worrying self. She was concerned that the neighbor's doors banged loudly while she was trying to sit and read. She wanted to know how much it would cost to fix their doors so they wouldn't bother her.

When I'd talk to her, I would see in her eyes that she wasn't happy at all. She thought that these external issues *were* her problem and completely missed the real point. She needed an identity shift so that she could positively engage her world, her neighbors, and her opportunities. Sue wasn't truly living. She was just waiting around to die. And she was blind to the misery she created for herself. (I adore this woman and recently found an opportunity to talk with her about discovering purpose in her life. After a few questions to clarify the benefits, her new journey toward purpose has now begun!)

I see it so often with retirees. They aren't really retiring *to* something. They are retiring *from* something. And that something usually contains a good piece of their identity and self-worth, their purpose. We are all wired for purpose. We all seek significance. We all choose where we will find it.

The choice goes beyond obstacle or opportunity. The choice is whether you choose to live or not. What does it look like to live more fully? Simple. You positively, proactively engage your purpose. Look in the eyes of someone who is truly living and you will see fire and passion. You will see drive and the willingness to take the risks necessary to reach for the prize. Sometimes you will even feel the boundless energy they emanate. Often it is these people who have a hard time with pointless small-talk. They want deeper conversation.

Look in the eyes of someone like Tony Robbins or Oprah Winfrey and you will see what I mean. Truly living is not about wealth or position of prominence (though these often follow). It's not about your ability to get other people to follow you, vote for you, or even listen to your loud voice. It is about passion. Passion is a choice. Passion is life. Find your passion. Pursue your passion and you are pursuing a worthwhile purpose and, therefore, a worthwhile life. You are truly living.

3. Ignorance is Bliss

Ignorance is bliss . . . until it's not. Then it's a pure, living Hell! Many people I've met over the years were late to realize the effect their habits had on their health (smoking, weight gain, diabetes, refusal to go to the doctor that lead to cancer spreading virtually out of control), their relationships (spouse having an affair, children bullied at school who attempt suicide, friends struggling with major challenges, refusal to accept that parents are aging), and their finances (overspending, poor income stream, dead-end jobs, failure to launch an effective career, refusal to answer the phone to talk to creditors).

At the time, it feels like bliss. It's far from it. When you focus only on the short-term satisfactions and feeling good *now—*failing to recognize the needs and importance of relationships and maintaining good health and financial footings—you end up unhealthy, broke, and alone. Many people reach the end of their lives in this way. Their purpose, if you can call it that, was to please themselves and sate their desires without regard for the long-term consequences—especially the impact their choices would have on others.

Is there an area of your life where you are blissfully ignorant? Do you make decisions based solely on what makes you feel good right now? Perhaps it's your favorite beverage or food.

Maybe you've decided you will start exercising in the future. You might look at your spending and think you really do need all of that stuff. Do you *need* it or do you *want* it? There is a difference.

When we know the truth and don't follow it, we're lying to ourselves. When we say that we'll eat right, exercise more, spend less after the New Year, and then we don't do it, we've eroded the trust we have in ourselves. Once we begin to erode this trust by making empty promises to ourselves, we feel like a fraud. We start to believe one of two things. Either we believe that we are unworthy of accomplishment because we realize it was our own fault, or we shift blame elsewhere.

If you have creditors calling you for money, is it because they like harassing you, or because you couldn't resist living in a house or apartment far larger than you could afford, driving a nicer car than you could afford, maxing out your credit cards? Though sometimes bad things do happen to good people, much of the time these bad things are merely the consequences of an accumulation of bad choices.

How do people who are living their purpose react when bad things happen? They find opportunity and the lessons in it and use these to move themselves forward.

Bad *Day* or Bad *Choices*?

Let's take a look at a hypothetical scenario in which a man has lost his job. He walks into work one day, only to be told that he's fired. He's not laid off, just fired. In fact, there is a HELP WANTED sign in the front window that wasn't there when he left yesterday.

What a horrible boss he must have! He storms out, furious that he just got screwed over by "the man" again. Why do these jerks get put in charge, anyway? They never like him. The last few jobs he had were much the same. The first time it happened, he had a knot in the pit of his stomach that didn't go away for days. It wasn't until he "realized" that it wasn't his fault that it finally went away. The company always "got the gold mine" and he always "got the shaft"!

Let's go back in time just one day. Our friend arrives to work at 8:25 a.m., which is better than his normal day when he arrives shortly after 9. He is supposed to be there at 8 o'clock, ready to start working. After about an hour, he slips out the back door to take a 30-minute break. When he comes back in, he is greeted by another coworker who asks for help on a small task that will only take a few minutes. He declines to help and says that no one ever helps him when he needs it. "In fact," he says, "I should be making a lot more money here, since I do most of the work."

When called into his boss's office to review a project for which he is responsible, he makes excuses as to why it isn't finished and rolls his eyes when his boss asks him why. It's obvious to our friend that it's the supplier's fault—and the client doesn't really care that much, anyway! Feeling like he's been put through the ringer enough for the day, he decides to give himself some paid leave and walks out to take his lunch break. He doesn't return until the next morning, when he is "unexpectedly" fired.

How would you feel if this were your employee? Most employers wouldn't put up with this treatment, either. In fact, most probably wait far too long to fire someone like this. They are cancerous to any organization. It may not even be a work environment—it may be a personal relationship. These cancerous, toxic people live in ignorance, *willful* ignorance, of why they get nowhere in life. That knot that our friend felt in his stomach the first time he was fired was there to tell him something, and he chose to ignore it.

His conscience was telling him that he needed to wake up to his behaviors and make substantive changes. Instead of dealing with his own issues, he chose to force them onto others. He would not take any blame. His ignorance is bliss . . . until it's not. Now no one will hire him and he doesn't have much of a life at all. Having no purpose is the epitome of a pure, living Hell. You go nowhere—slowly or quickly, it's all the same.

Creating Your Own Kryptonite

We have a family friend who has been an inspiration to us in many ways. We adore him and his wife. They have wonderful empathy and care so deeply for others, which he has made into a career. As a couple, they give of their time, energy, and money to help others in need. Their passion is obvious. Their purpose is Godly and clear.

And yet, despite it all, he creates his own Kryptonite. Jim has long, scraggly hair. When people don't like him or he fails to connect with people, he has a ready excuse that they don't like how he looks.

If it is suggested that he cut his hair if he feels they are the issue, he gets angry and says that they need to be more open-minded and leave him alone. Jim has created a self-limiting "look" so that he doesn't need to address other underlying issues that are far more personal in nature. His hair has become a shield which he uses to deflect the truth of any other issues he faces. It is his choice to keep it. He chooses to carry his Kryptonite with him.

Haircuts, colors, and scraggly beards aside, many people create other self-limiting factors in their lives. It goes beyond physical appearance. There are generally three areas in which people make self-limiting choices, or Kryptonite.

1. Appearance

2. Words

3. Actions

At first, many of us don't even realize that we are limiting our potential with our choices. Often it's because we aren't even aware that it's a choice at all. Years ago, during a meeting, I made a sarcastic comment about something pretty unimportant. A man who later became my mentor pulled me aside after the meeting to give me valuable advice.

He told me that there is no room for sarcasm in the life of a leader. I had potential that he would love to see developed, and he had learned that lesson about sarcasm himself the hard way. It has occurred to me in the years since then that there are many ways that we verbally limit ourselves. Now, I am aware of the choices I make simply with the words I choose to use.

Most people have heard of the importance of positive self-talk. Though that is important, it's not what I'm talking about. Cursing, name-calling, and gossip are clearly ways to limit your success. Other Kryptonite in this area includes poor grammar and spelling, talking only about yourself, dominating conversations by not letting others speak, taking credit that is not yours to take, and placing blame on others. It never ceases to amaze me how many people *know* that these limit the level of their success but are virtually belligerent about it. They have made the choice to limit themselves.

Actions are often another source of Kryptonite. In today's world of over-sharing through social media, people are surprised when they lose out on jobs because of what they share in such forums as Facebook. Make no mistake—any good employer is going to check for you online as well as asking for references and checking those. If you make poor choices that get back to your workplace, someone will know and it may limit or end your career progression.

Even far less severe actions, such as being late to work and meetings, procrastinating on projects, and getting others to do your work for you, can be very limiting. We do not live in a vacuum. What we say and do is heard and seen. When you are late to meetings routinely, people expect less of you. When your projects are lackluster and done at the last minute, people don't feel they can count on you. They doubt you.

Creating your own Kryptonite is your own choice. Self-limiting choices will mean that your powers will likely never reach the status of "Super." If you choose not to look the part, sound the part, or act the part, don't ever expect to be cast in the role of a Super-*anything*. Your potential and your trajectory are limited.

You might be thinking that it's wrong to be limited in this way. That doesn't mean it's not true. Ask yourself, whether you see it in yourself or others, what else is behind this self-limiting choice? There is usually some underlying issue or insecurity. Deal with that and your Super Power becomes super-possible.

Wrong Choices vs. Bad Choices

Have you ever stopped to consider the difference between a wrong choice and a bad choice? *Wrong* is the opposite of *right*. *Bad* is the opposite of *good*. Wouldn't we all like to make choices that are both right and good? Of course we would! Is it always possible? Perhaps, but it isn't at all common. Let me illustrate the difference between *wrong* and *bad*. They are typically at opposite ends of the poor-choice continuum.

In making a wrong choice, irreparable damage can be done. In some cases, it can also be deemed as highly immoral. An extreme example would be Hitler's decision to exterminate the Jewish people. Irreparable, immoral, and very, very wrong. Less severe wrong choices are made every day. Even when the damage isn't irreparable, it is often very hard to correct. Choosing to do harm—physically, emotionally, or spiritually—

to others is a wrong choice. It is a wrong choice to do this to yourself as well.

For most of us, we realize that these choices are wrong. Wrong choices are pretty easy to identify.

A bad choice, on the other hand, is usually less severe. Your friend or loved one who is on a diet is coming over and you make a big, gooey chocolate cake for them. Not nice! You don't receive the promotion at work and lash out by gossiping about how unqualified the person is who was promoted instead of you. You know that you should get started on this big project, but it's easier to procrastinate since the deadline is months away. You can't help but buy that new pair of shoes and put it on the credit card, even though you can't really afford them now.

Bad choices, when taken individually, don't destroy. When taken as a whole, however, they accumulate to produce negative consequences. The sum total of bad choices can destroy a person's credibility and chances of success at work (gossiping and procrastination) and distance them from friends (passive-aggressively making that cake).

When others look at your choices, what decision framework do they see? What do you see? Is it that you take the path of least resistance (also viewed as lazy)? Do you put off until tomorrow what really should be done today? Are you selfish? When you RSVP for an event and back out because something else (i.e. something better, or you just don't feel like attending) came along, how likely are you to be included in the future? Do you realize that people are watching?

4. Myths and Rationalizations About Choice

There are several myths and rationalizations about the choices we make. To be able to make consistently good choices, we need to address a few of these myths. Before we do, it's important to understand a key difference between an average person—one who has difficulty committing to anything for very long—and an achiever.

The Planner

An average person, at best, is a planner. They look ahead to something they want to change in themselves. They plan to start this new habit next week, next month, or next year. A good example would be the droves of people who start January 1st each year with the goal of "getting in shape." They plan it out. They buy the new outfits for their workouts, get a cool new pair of exercise shoes, sign up at a gym or for an online workout program. They may even tell everyone that, as of January 1st, they are going to finally get in shape.

The plan, at first glance, looks solid. And it would be, if not for the normalcy of past habits and other predictable obstacles. On January 15th, with the new habit not fully in place yet, the average person encounters an obstacle—the common cold. After recovering a week later, they may head back to workout-land or they may not. The limited progress they have seen is gone. The excitement and euphoria of this new adventure is extinguished. They may work out a couple more times, but we already know it won't last. They know it too. So they quit . . . over and over, every year.

The Strategist

An achiever, on the other hand, does some of the same planning, but they take it a few steps further. They look at the *what-ifs* that can happen. They strategize ways to overcome the obstacles. In fact, they expect them. They don't wait until next Monday, next month, or next year to get started. They just start, with an experimenter's Strategic Mindset. They know it won't be perfect initially, but they are okay with that. They will learn and adapt as they go.

If, two weeks into the workout routine, they develop a cold, it doesn't derail their progress. They deal with the cold, have a set of exercises that keeps their body on the right track so they can continue to make progress during their illness.

They have already found a solid accountability partner— perhaps a dedicated friend, mentor, or personal trainer—who holds them accountable for returning to their full routine as soon as they can. They know which of their friends can be trusted to provide true accountability.

They make tremendous progress. They are the ones who actually achieve greater success in whatever they endeavor to do.

Planner vs. Strategist

The average person lies to themselves by believing it will be easier than it is. They believe that they have done all the right things by setting a start date, telling people about their new goal, and being prepared. The truth is that, without a CONTINGENCY Mindset, they set themselves up for failure before they even begin.

The achiever knows there will be obstacles that get in the way. They know that the road won't be easy. They don't need to shout their intentions to the world. They only need a select few trusted people who will hold them accountable to follow through on their pledge.

They think ahead to several *if-then* scenarios.

- If I get sick, then I will continue to do as much as I can to stay in my routine.

- If I am called away because of work, family, or anything else, then I will make sure to stay at or find somewhere to continue my workout routine.

- If I can't find somewhere, I have several online resources lined up where I can get a workout by simply following along via tablet or smartphone.

- If I start to get stale or bored with my workout, I will hire a personal trainer and have budgeted time and money for that already.

- Regardless of where I am or how I feel, I commit to checking in with my accountability partner on a daily basis.

- If I fail to do so, then I will do an additional 50 burpees the following day.

That, my friends, is how a STRATEGIST works. Even though all of the possible obstacles aren't known in advance, a strategist lives with a Contingency Mindset. When an obstacle arises, they are mentally prepared to think and plan past it.

This doesn't just work for developing and staying with an exercise routine. It works extremely well for any goal or objective you may have. This is how I structure investment and retirement goals for clients. Want to make a permanent change in some area of your life and are truly committed to it? Become a strategist. It works.

Lies and Excuses

As we discuss the myths and rationalizations that follow, try to keep your Strategic Mindset firmly in place. You will see more clearly that the myths are not truths; they are lies. Rationalizations are not reasons; they are excuses.

#1: "It's no big deal."

If it's really no big deal, you wouldn't have any trouble making a good choice. From the example above, the "It's no big deal" lie is skipping a day of your workout or getting a banana split afterward because you "deserve it." Have you ever noticed how many people reward themselves with the same behavior they are trying to change? "I've done really well eating healthy this week, so I have earned that bag of cookies." "I'm feeling so energized and invigorated from exercising all week that I'm going to give myself the weekend to do nothing." These are the natural result of the "It's no big deal" lie.

When you hear yourself justifying a choice with "It's no big deal," remember that this is code for self-destruction. It's far more insidious than skipping workouts and having banana splits. This is the same logic used by the people who created the 2008–09 financial crisis in the United States and around the world that evaporated the retirement savings of countless individuals. Translation: It is a big deal!

#2: "It's too hard."

If it's too hard, then you haven't been planning and strategizing how to eat the proverbial elephant one bite at a time. No meaningful goal, result, or objective is too hard if we break it down into its component parts. The "It's too hard" lie is a complete cop-out. It tells the story that you were never committed to the decision in the first place. The choices we make that will grow, develop, and shape us over the years are not supposed to be easy. But they can be manageable.

Was it too hard for Oprah to start her own company in a media world flooded with competitors and become one of the most influential women in the world? Do you know her story? If not, look it up. Then tell me making a choice about passing up the banana split is too hard. Know that it will be challenging and plan your way through and around it with a Contingency Mindset. Be a strategist.

#3: "It's not worth it."

Let's change this one to read what people really mean: "*I'm not worth it.*" This is one of the most self-deprecating excuses you could make. It screams to the world that you choose to maintain your low regard for yourself, have no desire or intention to improve, and are determined to stay the way you are—a loser. It says that you don't value yourself. What it means to the rest of us is that you don't think we should value you very highly, either. Drop this one flat on its face, because you *are* worth it.

This is just a small sample of the lies and excuses we tell ourselves. What do you say and think to rationalize the choices you make? Think carefully about the last time you had a goal and gave up on achieving it. What did you say to yourself? Find the flaws in it. That's what a strategist does. It is how we *respond* that will either allow us to grow into our Super-selves or stay where we've always been.

Moments of Maturity

A common belief is that maturity happens over time, as we age. I would argue that nothing could be further from the truth. Have you ever met a person in their forties or fifties who acts like a child, with very little filter on their words and actions? These are self-limiting behaviors. Or perhaps you've met a twelve-year-old who blows you away with how "grown up" they seem? I certainly have. Witnessing these differences has forced me to challenge my long-held belief that we become more mentally and emotionally mature as we get older.

In observing people of various ages who seem to have matured at different rates, I've found one major commonality: choice. There are many moments in all of our lives that force us to make a decision about how something will affect us. At those times, we can make a maturing choice or a choice to remain stagnant. I call these "moments of maturity."

I met a twelve-year-old who seemed remarkably mature for her age. I didn't think much of it initially. After all, they say girls mature faster than boys, right? In talking to her and her grandmother, I found out that she'd had a very tough life early on. Early on? She's only twelve! Exactly. By the age of twelve, she had been abused by a family member, witnessed the divorce of her parents, drug abuse by her mother, and was now living with her grandparents.

She didn't realize it, but it was her response to these events that matured her at a young age. It was the choice she made. Her younger brother made a different choice and seemed far too immature for his age. She had chosen to take on the role of "mother" when necessary and to sacrifice herself to abuse to save him from it.

Though an extreme example, and one I would never wish on anyone, it points to maturity developing in those moments of choice, making them moments of maturity. She made maturing choices in how she handled what was happening to her and around her. These moments happen to us more times than we likely realize. You hear a few words of advice from a trusted colleague about sarcasm being the Kryptonite of leadership potential. How do you react or respond?

The choice you make has the potential of enhancing your business and leadership potential. You offer to pray for a friend undergoing hardship and fail to do it. This also is a maturing choice. Can you be trusted? Can you even trust yourself? Or are you forming your identity and maturity around empty promises?

On the other end of the spectrum are adults who haven't matured as much as we might expect. They are pretty easy to spot in the crowd and, sadly, their numbers are vast. They are people who have few filters. I call it "diarrhea of the mouth." Whatever thought pops into their head comes rushing straight out of their mouth with little if any delay.

On social media, they are easy to spot. They are the ones always complaining and tearing others down, seemingly without regard for the impact it could have. In the workplace, they are the ones who have self-limited careers. Regardless of their skill-set, there's really only so high they can go. When opportunities to mature arise, they make the choice that leaves them immature—failing to rise to new standards.

They blame others instead of taking ownership for what they did or did not do. Even when they do take ownership, they fail to take the steps necessary to correct the issue or to ensure that it doesn't happen again. Many of us have at least heard comments about people with self-limiting careers. Haven't heard the comments? Then it could be you.

There is a silver lining. It is never too late to start making choices that help you mature and grow. These choices help you see the truth behind the myths and rationalizations. It is an awakening.

PTSD vs. PTG

One person who undergoes immense pain and torment from events in their lives becomes cold and bitter. Another uses this to launch themselves on a very positive trajectory. The history books and bookstores are full of stories of those who chose to overcome their circumstances to reach tremendous heights. Those who became cold and bitter are mostly forgotten. Why the difference? Simple. It's the choice between PTG and PTSD.

Most of us have heard of post-traumatic stress disorder (PTSD), and many have suffered from it in some way. The term originally began as an explanation of the effects of combat on soldiers. Back in the early years of the last century, it was referred to as "shell shock." Without going into a detailed history of the terms, the extreme nature of the original intent of the term PTSD is sometimes lost or overlooked. I do not intend to marginalize or minimize the extreme suffering by combat veterans. I am utilizing the milder form of PTSD here, though I have seen people overcome the most extreme versions as well.

Today, people who have never seen the field of combat who may have suffered some psychological trauma, ranging anywhere from an auto accident to weathering the 2008–09 financial crisis to severe abuse, are labeled with PTSD.

We all have issues. None of us are immune. Whether you have ADD, OCD, PTSD, or any of a myriad of other issues, being successful is well within your grasp.

Here is how I define successful people:

Successful people own their neuroses, pack them in their luggage, and proudly carry them through life. They put down their luggage (full of their own issues) and stand on top of it to reach greater heights.

These are the people who, though often diagnosed early on as having PTSD, choose not to let it hold them back. They choose post-traumatic *growth*, or PTG, instead. We've all heard of people who had a bad childhood, were assaulted as an adult, or lost everything and declared bankruptcy, only to rise from the ashes like a phoenix to soar over it all.

They chose to learn and not view their life and identity as that of a failure. In the end, they chose their identity with great intentionality and did not allow the world or circumstances to choose it for them.

5. Welcome to an Awakening of Awareness

Most of us move through life largely in the fog of doing what we've always done, simply because it's what we've always done. We believe change is bad, even painful. We fight either for the status quo or a return to the "good ol' days." Frankly, many people are blissfully unaware (remember—"ignorance is bliss") that they are even making choices at all.

Failure to make an active, intentional choice is a choice in itself. It's making a choice by default, which is rarely optimal. Hopefully by now, you know a few of the pitfalls of failing to make proactive, intentional choices. You have become aware of a myriad of choices, large and small, that can have dramatic impacts on your life and the lives of your family members for years to come. Here are just a few examples:

- Choosing to go out to eat many evenings because it's easier than preparing a meal and you're tired. In the long term, it's unhealthy for you and your family, is a real drain on family finances, and teaches your children to live by convenience (and maybe that every meal should come with a junk toy!).

- *OR* opting instead to plan your meals ahead so that it's still easy and convenient. It's also healthier.

    - Costs: fewer relationships with workers at the drive-through window, some time on a weekend to plan and prepare meals.

    - Results: far less expensive and will take much less time if planned ahead (think freezer meals, for example).

- Choosing a college degree (or encouraging someone else to) without being fully aware of important factors like aptitude, workload involved in getting the degree, job prospects after graduation, debt load likely to be created. Long-term side effects include being a slave to a paycheck and student-loan debt, poor job opportunities, and possibly being part of the boomerang generation living at home again with parents.

    - *OR* planning ahead, doing aptitude tests, job-shadowing and interviewing people who are currently in those careers at different stages, sitting down and taking ownership of the degree track and pre-planning an entire college course load before college even begins.

        - Costs: time and energy at the outset to ensure that wise choices are made in a well thought-out, intentional manner.

- Results: possibly less time in school, greater clarity in the vision and destination, building habits around how to approach choices with purpose, lower college debt, increased confidence, and lower likelihood of switching majors frequently and subjecting yourself to repeated failures.

- Choosing to sleep in until the last possible moment. This often results in unhealthy morning meals, feeling frazzled during the day, short tempers, never being fully centered and able to stay on course, and lack of focus and attention to detail.

  - *OR* getting over the belief that you're not a morning person or that mornings are for relaxation; choosing to *become* a morning person or to be more productive and proactive with your mornings.

    - Costs: to get adequate sleep, you may need to go to bed earlier and stop hitting the snooze button.

    - Results: better energy throughout the day; being more calm, centered, and focused; and choosing to get the most important parts of your day addressed early so that you can have much more enjoyment of every opportunity each day brings. You will also be much more able to find, seek, and even create opportunities each day.

These are just a few examples of choices and only a few consequences of each. Now that you are aware that choices surround us at all times, you have the tremendous opportunity to approach those choices with greater levels of intentionality. Your eyes are opening and will continue to see and identify the choices you have. Welcome to an awakening of awareness. Never again will you be able to take choices lightly.

Choose wisely, my friends. Each choice is like a musical note. Through deliberate choice, you can create a beautiful song as you move through your life. How does your current song sound? Is it pleasing to the ears? Or is it more like a screeching banshee or a funeral dirge?

Though many of us believe that some people, from Mozart to Tiger Woods, were born with natural talent, that's not necessarily true. Mozart's father was a music teacher and invested countless hours in helping to grow and nurture his remarkably young son's interest in music into amazing talent.

Tiger Woods, similarly, chose to pursue his passion for golf from an early age, immediately put in immense practice time, and continues to do so today. Both of these men are often mistaken for being "naturals," and yet, while their immense talent is not at all in question, they did not choose to sit back and rely on talent alone. They knew the importance of hard work in developing and honing their skills and abilities.

Like them, you have the choice to develop yourself in important areas. You choose which areas you want to enhance in your life and how you do so. That can be a powerful choice, which is why many people struggle with where to start. I would argue that where to start is far less important than *when* to start.

When to start is *NOW*. As my husband frequently says, "Adults decide; children don't." Be the adult and simply choose one thing to do to start improving your life today. It could be something sparked by a concept in this book, another book, or something that's been on your heart for years. It doesn't really matter.

The key is to get out of the starting gate. Otherwise, you'll never reach the finish line. You can always add, change, grow, and improve as you go through the race. What's your choice for getting out of that starting gate?

If you need a little help, perhaps a few suggestions, check out the workbook at www.chooseyoursuperpower.com for ideas on how to get started. Then go to the CYSP Community at The Super Guild on Facebook to share with us what area you chose to start!

6. Your New Autonomy

It is often in the depths of the abyss that we find our true selves. When we are shaken, what we're full of spills out. When squeezed, are you sweet like an orange or sour like a lemon? Enough with the metaphors. You should be getting the idea.

Brilliance and success rarely come without a cost. That cost often includes being ridiculed and misunderstood, at least by some. The path is neither straight nor smooth. Developing autonomy is the key, the first step in developing a Super Power. Without this it is nearly impossible to design, develop, and deploy your purpose. All Superheroes go through the struggle of figuring out this step.

Let me repeat the Merriam-Webster Dictionary's definition of autonomy. "1: the quality or state of being self-governing; 2: self-directing freedom and especially moral independence."

First, it is a *state* of being. Your state is your choice. Choice is a foundational concept. Without knowing and understanding both the short-and long-term consequences of your choices, it is unlikely that you will develop the level of autonomy needed to reach for your potential.

Second, it requires *self*-governing and *self*-directing freedom. Choices are up to you to make—no one else. Intentionality of your choices shows your ability to self-govern and, ultimately, your ability to self-direct your own freedom. If you merely follow the norms of society or someone else, you're part of the herd. Only when you begin self-directing your freedom and practicing self-governance will you rise above the rest.

Finally, it involves "moral independence." Morals and values should be aligned with the choices you make to keep you in a state of self-directed freedom. Purpose is interwoven with your values and ensures the best chance of success in remaining morally independent.

Moral independence cannot be achieved when following the norms of others and their broken moral compasses. It must be independent and uninfluenced by them. Your moral code is separated from the rationalizations made by average people, and you hold yourself to a more consistent moral code of ethics. Develop your autonomy—guided by your own moral compass—and you are ready to define and develop your purpose.

Calibrating Your Moral Compass

What is your moral compass? Does it seem a little vague and hazy at this point? For many of us, our morals have been woven through the fabric of social norms for so long that they are difficult to identify. In order to uncover what your personal moral compass looks like, make a list of your "non-negotiables." What are the things you would never do, no matter the circumstances? Murder, theft, verbally or physically abusing someone, etc.

Some seem pretty obvious, and that's okay. Start there. Once you've reached more ambiguous ground, keep weaving your way through your life experiences. What have you seen others do that you would not? Perhaps you recall choices you made in the past that you would not consider making now? Keep weaving your way through this list. You can include things like smoking, drinking, cursing, yelling, and many others. Go from the big, obvious stuff down to the daily choices that may seem pretty small and insignificant.

Choices have a compounding effect and are rarely inconsequential. For a more full list and examples, check out the workbook at www.chooseyoursuperpower.com.

You are drawing a line in the sand. You decide which behaviors, activities, and attitudes you will and will not tolerate in yourself. You need clarity with your moral compass, because you are about to choose your Super Power.

PART 2

Purpose

You were created to be unique and to have purpose. Yet many people today merely float through life drowning in a sea of self-made mediocrity. Some can tell you a vague purpose, a few have a very clear life purpose, and still others can tell you nothing at all. "What is your life purpose?" The question may bring yearning, tears, or anger, but rarely apathy. We were created to have a purpose, and we know it. Now your task is to identify your own. In this section, we will define, design, and begin to deploy your purpose.

7. Super-Purpose Begins

Your Super Power is found in your purpose. What makes it *Super* is the amount of dedication you put toward it. Many people have a purpose that they can rattle off to anyone who asks. It usually sounds a lot like a job title. "My purpose is to make money for my clients." "My purpose is to create client satisfaction and retention." "My purpose is to preach the word of God to the congregation." Are these wrong or bad purposes? Not at all! Are they really *Super*? That depends on what else there is to that purpose. Let's take a look at a couple of these.

"My purpose is to make money for my clients."

This could be good if you are his client and that is your sole objective. However, in digging deeper, we need to find out why they want more money. Making money so that you can spend lavishly on yourself to make others jealous is far different than if your purpose is to be charitably minded and use it to help others.

What about the purpose of the person making the statement? Is his real purpose helping clients be able to retire with dignity, or just making them enough money (and himself far more) so that they will leave their money with him? There are many other questions that could be asked as well. The key is that the *meaning* behind the purpose matters just as much as the words.

"My purpose is to preach the word of God to the congregation."

What congregation? Just the ones who come to visit you on Sunday mornings? What if they have needs outside of what you provide in your sermons? Perhaps there are people outside of your church who are desperate to hear your message. Do you share it with them, too?

I could go on with examples of incomplete purposes. I won't. What I hope you realize is that the rest of the story, as Paul Harvey would say, is at least as important, or more so, as what you list as a job title—this defines your purpose. When you state a purpose that sounds like a job title, you are leaving out detail. It's the detail that matters the most. Without it, your beliefs and values are missing. Usually, it is merely a part of your overall purpose—perhaps a mission within it.

What is your purpose? How do you find it? What's the path to discovery and enlightenment when it comes to purpose? The journey is yours. As mentioned in the section on Butterflies and Moths, it is closely related to how you see yourself contributing to your own growth and possibly to the development of others.

Your purpose will change, morph, and evolve over time as you fine-tune your personal gifts, abilities, and aptitudes. You start with looking at the choices you've made and doing an honest evaluation.

Choices and Purpose

The choices you make and your feelings about them are a good place to start looking at your purpose. Choices can either keep us in our comfort zone or push us past it. How does it feel? For me, too long in my comfort zone makes me numb. Too far *out* of my comfort zone and I feel like I'm about to pass out! I love the term "massage your discomfort zone" from George Mumford in *The Mindful Athlete*.

What choices have made you feel positive, powerful, and purposeful? What preceded those choices? Was there any discomfort there? How did you feel afterward? Relive a few of those choices and the feelings they evoke.

You shape and mold your own identity. You choose it, just like you choose your purpose. Your identity doesn't choose you, unless you let the world define you.

If you could have a "do-over," what choices would you make differently? What lessons did your bad choices teach you? How did you know they were bad choices? I know that hindsight is 2020, and that's what I'm counting on.

Launching the Super Power Search

It starts with purpose. Determining your purpose is a choice and, like most choices, it gives you the opportunity to make lasting impact. For most of my life I got much of this backward. This book is really my own journey of self-discovery shared with others.

I mistakenly believed that reaching my goals was my purpose. Were they really my goals? Or were they what I thought others wanted or expected of me? I bought into the premise of raising my goal once it was within reach. So I rarely reached my goals. I set myself up to never feel fulfilled in accomplishing my goals, which I believed was my purpose.

Since I thought my goals gave me purpose, I would begin to feel rejected by my own purpose and would go into a mental fog. Being the resilient type, I would inevitably rally myself to set a new list of goals to accomplish and set off happily trying to achieve these. I did achieve my goals on occasion, but it was not the same as achieving my *purpose*.

There were two problems. First, I would raise them to unsustainable levels before actually reaching them and suffer a backslide. This is like being the kid in the backseat of the car asking, "Are we there yet?" I knew the answer would always be *NO*.

Second, my losses would weigh on me far more heavily than my wins. I would veer off course. I didn't realize that I needed an Experimenter's Mindset. I needed to view it as a data point and learn from it. Failure felt far too personal.

I made excuses, lots of excuses. "It's not important anyway." "That wasn't my real goal." "I have so much going now. I'll need to try again later." "My husband and kids need my attention. Why can't I get any help at home?" "This is too hard/too much for one woman to do/too low on my priority list." I could go on for pages, but you should get the point by now.

Why couldn't I be the achiever as I saw others being? Were they making sacrifices that I didn't see or understand? What would I have to sacrifice to reach my goals? What I kept going back to was the simple fact that others seemed to have some sort of superhuman powers and I had none. I wanted to have these Super Powers too. But how?

Starting with the end in mind, I began the journey of figuring out how to gain my own Super Powers. Of course, the obvious question revolves around which Super Powers you want. Does it really matter? Absolutely! If you develop in the area that is wrong for you, you still won't feel fulfilled. You will be aimed in the wrong direction.

I am an avid target shooter as well as martial artist and very amateur dirt-biker. I know a lot about aiming in the right direction. Humans are very target-oriented people (a.k.a. teleological). A perfect example is the concept of target fixation.

Target Fixation

I find the issue of target fixation everywhere in my life. It's probably much like buying a car. You find the perfect car, just unique and unusual enough you can't find it in the store parking lot . . . until you show up at the store and see three or four more just like it in the lot. You might even notice a few with the same "unique" color within a few days. Once we are aware of something and its importance is known, we see it everywhere. That's target fixation.

Target fixation is also our uncanny ability to achieve or zero in on whatever has our focus, and the more intense our focus the more likely we are to get there. Have you ever been driving and look off to your right at something and find the car moving slightly in that direction? That's target fixation.

Our family enjoys dirt-biking, and this is probably where I've physically noticed target fixation the most keenly. While on the trails, if you focus on *not* hitting the tree, you hit the tree. Why? Because that's where your focus, or fixation, is. I would know. I've hit a lot of trees. Thankfully I don't go very fast. I've also wrecked on tiny rocks and tree roots that should have been easy to maneuver. It's an apt metaphor for focusing on the wrong thing and allowing our attention to be diverted from what's really important. Sometimes target fixation hurts— especially my pride.

Realizing that there had to be an opportunity for learning in there somewhere, I listened to my brilliant husband. He told me, "Focus on where you want to go instead of where you don't." Sounds simple and brilliant until you are on the bike and that tree is there.

If you were a little fly inside my helmet, you'd still hear me talking to myself, saying things like, "Focus through. Look ahead. Eyes follow the bend in the path." By focusing on where I want to be, those other obstacles just disappear. I still hit the rocks and roots. But I have faith that the bike will take me over them and get me to where I'm focused.

This logic follows also with shooting. Who wants to be around the shooter who doesn't look where they're shooting? I sure don't!

Have you ever met the parent so concerned that their child not "mess up" in some area that their focus actually leads the child directly to that behavior? Drugs, self-centeredness, bullying, and despising their parents are all examples that come to mind. The parents are so fixated on the obstacle, which causes their children to be fixated on it as well, that they often hit it head on at tremendous speed. What a wreck!

So if we focus on what and who we do not want to become through our life's journey, that's exactly where we will land. This is a way to become the Super-*villain* instead of the Super*hero*.

Where are your sights set? Just like you'd want to take careful aim at a paper target in front of you at the gun range, you should choose your target carefully here as well. Ask yourself positive questions and drill down in those areas. Do your long-, intermediate-, and short-term goals all line up?

Aligning with Your Purpose

In shooting pistols and rifles, you have a front sight and a rear sight. Think of the rear sight (closest to you) as your short-term goal, your front sight (at the end of the firearm) as the intermediate-term goal, and the bullseye out there as your long-term goal.

Are they lined up? If the front and rear sights aren't lined up with the target, where do you think your round will hit? It won't hit the bullseye, that's for sure. The great news is that noticing this early on creates an opportunity. By making very small adjustments to the alignment of your front and rear sights and focusing on your fundamentals (which we will discuss in a future chapter), you can drastically change the trajectory and get yourself onto the correct path very quickly and simply.

The same is true for you as you set your sights on what you choose to accomplish and who you choose to be. Defining your purpose more fully helps you to zero in on what it will take to become and do more than you ever thought possible. The key is to have good vision. If you can't see the target clearly (like the bullseye), you will be shooting blind. And that never ends well for anyone.

Don't be the type of person who says, "Goals aren't important." I've met those people. They live sad, unfulfilled lives. The only blessing is that most of them have no idea what greatness they are missing—"ignorance is bliss." But we are all wired and created for goals and purpose. Find yours.

Step one: open your eyes.

The Breakdown

Eyes Open

Let's break this down into simple components. First, keep your eyes open. If you close your eyes or focus on not hitting the tree, you will still hit the tree.

Can you see clearly past the short-and intermediate-term goals? In a practical sense, you need to remind yourself of why and what you are trying to ultimately accomplish. Those shorter-term goals are merely waypoints to getting you to the much more fulfilling end—your purpose.

Maintain focus on where you want to be, and remember to maintain your Strategic Mindset.

Sights Aligned

Next, as you achieve (or even fail to achieve) the short-and intermediate-term goals, you need to see if those goals are what will still get you closer to fulfilling your ultimate purpose. If you do this early and frequently in the process and make it a common practice, you only need to make very small adjustments to correct your trajectory.

If you wait to do this after several months, years, or decades, you have lost valuable time that can never be regained and have also built bad habits. Make sure your sights are aligned on a consistent, intentional basis. I call this "verification on target."

Since your eyes can only focus clearly on one distance at a time, it may take a while to analyze your alignment. It has to be adjusted frequently. In fact, every time you take a "shot" at your target, you need to reevaluate.

Tunnel Vision (Focusing on Fewer Things)

Tunnel vision often gets a bad reputation. In this context, it means to focus on fewer things. Avoid distractions and focusing on too many targets at one time. These targets should build on one another, not compete for your focus. It also means maintaining focus on what you can control, not what you cannot control. You can control your actions, activities, and attitude. You cannot control what other people do and say and how they behave (i.e. how they choose to react to you). Stay on target.

I can control, for example, the alignment of my front and rear sights with the target as well as the basic fundamentals of sound shooting. Out of my control are things like wind, sudden noises that may distract me, misfires, and magazine capacity.

If I cannot control them, I must decide to either ignore them or compensate for them. That takes judgment to know which will actually pull me off target. If it's going to pull me off target, I compensate for them. Ignoring them won't help.

Purpose

Eyes open, sights aligned, and tunnel vision around your purpose means that your chances of success go up exponentially. You will hit your bullseye; you will fulfill your purpose.

Let's begin the search for our Super Powers. It begins with an awareness of choice and the concept of intentionality. The best life with the most purpose is a life forged through intentional choice.

8. Exploring Purpose

We frequently get advice telling us to focus on one thing at a time, or, at the very least, to narrow our focus. Overall, I find this helpful—but only once I have determined where my focus should be. Until you discover your passions and develop your purpose, it can be a scary and unproductive thought. You either feel pulled in all different directions or feel numb and stagnant. Being at either end of the spectrum and told to focus on one thing seems nearly impossible.

A good friend who sees the value in purpose and hears me talking about it all the time confessed that she's struggling because she has no purpose. Her purpose had been to keep her family going while her husband was out of work and injured several times over two years. He's finally better and working again. She is very thankful for the release of financial and emotional stresses now, but she feels she has no purpose and is floating through life rudderless. It's not the first time I've heard this. That numb feeling can make you cry. I get it.

At the opposite end of that spectrum is the person who feels that they have *too many* purposes and cannot possibly focus on any one. They are pulled through life by whichever emergency is hitting them now. They run from home to work to home, always putting out fires. Even though they often create this hectic lifestyle, that doesn't always make it any easier to manage.

They may even appear to "have it all together" and already have Super Powers. I thought they *did* have Super Powers. In many cases, I was wrong. They don't.

Or they may be the ones who roll in late consistently, looking like the frustrated mess they are. The truth is that—whether they look like a mess or super-powered—they're in much the same boat. The difference is that some are better illusionists than others. Confession time: that's me. Which one? It varies.

The Truth About the Journey

What you won't often hear is that we all have our own personal journeys to purpose. Most of the time it starts by *expanding* our horizons, not shrinking them. Whether we are caught up in the day-to-day hectic running around that we think is life or stumbling numbly in the dark seeking purpose, the first step is to expand, not shrink.

First, on the path of self-discovery, you need to be able to expand your mind, think, and dream big. Have you ever had a really big idea? How did it feel? Exciting? Overwhelming? Exhilarating? Captivating? Did you pursue it? What were the results? How would you like to live the thrill of that exhilaration on a much more consistent basis?

This, my friends, is what it feels like to be truly *ALIVE*! Find a passion, pursue a purpose, and you finally feel like you are living again. Get out and work hard to see all of the options; think outside yourself and your current situation. Put in the hard work necessary to weed out what doesn't suit you so that you can discover what does.

If you believe your passion is to build homes through Habitat for Humanity, go help on a few houses to see if you are right. It might turn out that it's not your passion, and getting involved in other areas of this great charity are more suited to you— perhaps working in a ReStore site. It's not a failure when you realize it's not your passion or purpose. It's a learning moment, a moment of maturity.

One of my clients, several years ago, said that antiquing was such a passion for her that she wanted to open an antique shop in her retirement years. She believed that was her new purpose. Before sinking the money into such an endeavor, I encouraged her to find a store already out there and work a few Saturdays each month—even as a volunteer—to get an idea of what it was like.

After two short months, she called to say that her passion for antiques was still there, while her desire to own a store was not. She grew annoyed and stressed by people who wanted to nickel-and-dime her on everything by arguing that the items (remember, these were *antiques*) were not in perfect condition. She now volunteers at a community health clinic for impoverished families without adequate healthcare resources. She has found her passion and purpose, but first, she explored several options before finding one suitable to her.

If you aren't sure where your true passion lies or you want to expand your horizons to experience other possibilities, make a list of some of those possibilities and start at the one you believe suits you best. It's not a failure if one or more isn't right for you. It's a learning point, nothing more. This journey can be fun and invigorating.

What if you have no idea where to start? *The key is just to start.* Ask friends, neighbors, coworkers, and family what they are interested in, where their passions are. When someone asks you to do something out of your norm, say YES (as long as you can do so without any long-term commitment or sense of obligation to continue doing it). When you discover that the endeavor is not your passion, no matter how worthy the cause may be, bow out of it. Have an exit strategy in mind before you get in so that you can graciously depart without hurt feelings.

I personally like to set a short time horizon of availability for them. "I am available to help on this project for two months. I will give you everything that I can for those two months and, at the end, will need to move on to other obligations."

If you decide it's a passion for you and you want to continue, they will be thrilled to have you! This can help keep you from becoming overwhelmed with a large number of activities, which is not the objective at all.

When I started as a financial advisor, I heard this all the time. "Get involved in every group you can. You will meet lots of potential clients that way." Did I? Yes. I was also involved in so many things that I couldn't focus on any of them sufficiently, which didn't leave a very good impression.

I eventually whittled it down to a very select few. If I'm elected to a board that allows for multiple terms (most people seem to go in intending to stay on the board as long as possible), I reevaluate my passion, purpose, and contribution near the end of each term. If I'm not passionate about it any longer, the group deserves to have someone involved who is. I would be doing a disservice by staying onboard.

Instead of feeling obligated to always say YES, now I immediately look to see if it fits with my purpose and is something that I'm passionate about. If not—or if I simply don't have the time for it at this point—I let them know, graciously, that I don't have the ability at this time to properly commit the needed time and energy to be of greatest service.

I thank them for the opportunity and for thinking of me. If it's something that I may want to do later, I make a point to tell them when I would be able to reconsider and have the time available. For many opportunities, now is not the right time. So the answer isn't always NO—it's "Not yet."

This has allowed me to zero in on those areas that help fulfill my purpose because I am passionate about them. It is my choice to accept or decline such invitations.

Sometimes, you have to expand your horizons and the base of experiences to be able to hone in on what "feeds" your purpose. You will find your passions through this type of exploration. Explore your options without getting locked into something long term, and I promise that you will find your passions and purpose. Finding and developing your Super Power starts with an amazing journey. Give yourself permission to embark on that journey.

This chapter underscores the importance of how you approach the development and deployment of your purpose. This is just a taste. The options you explore here will also give you the experiences you will need to complete the exercises in chapters 10 and 12.

9. Approaching Purpose

Purpose is a journey—complete with detours, traffic delays, beautiful vistas, and breathtaking memories. The detours and traffic delays often lead you to unexpected opportunities. You just need to be alert enough to see them. You won't always get it right and will sometimes deviate from your purpose. Your purpose may evolve throughout your life. That's normal.

The Experimenter's Mindset

The Growth Mindset, which includes looking for opportunities instead of obstacles, is essential as you begin to define and explore your purpose. It's just as important to have an Experimenter's Mindset. An experimenter is constantly trying new ways and combinations to see what works the best and, just as importantly, what doesn't work at all. Their emotions are not tied up in a failure.

Instead, an experimenter gets just as much valuable information from not getting the desired results as they do from getting the results they seek. They don't argue that some combination or experiment should work and keep trying to slam a square peg into a round hole. They simply shrug it off as the wrong peg for that hole, knowing it will be perfect if they find a square hole. They also know they can accomplish twice as much if they just find both a square hole and a round peg. That's how you live an optimal lifestyle.

It is nearly impossible to sustain a Growth Mindset without an Experimenter's Mindset. The two walk hand-in-hand. If you keep banging your head against a wall trying to make something work that never will, you miss countless other opportunities. You may eventually "win" at getting the square peg in the round hole, but at what cost? What growth might you have had if you would have instead spent your time and energy looking for the square hole and round peg?

Opportunities are everywhere. Just open your eyes and look. It takes an intentional choice and constantly reaffirming that choice to maintain a Growth Mindset. It's best accomplished when, like a scientist, you are able to chalk an experiment up to finding another way that didn't work as you march on past it to find what will work.

Many years ago, the 3M Company was looking to create a super-strong adhesive that would hold up to incredible amounts of weight and resistance. In one failed attempt, they achieved a lackluster result of an adhesive that was very mild and would only hold a light amount of weight for a short time. In fact, it took just the slightest tug to separate it because it typically failed to bond effectively to surfaces. They had a square peg and a round hole.

Failure? Not in the slightest. Created and launched in 1980, Post-it notes today generate over a billion dollars in sales per year. That square peg found its square hole, and the experimenters at 3M were still able to find the round peg in later experiments.

In what area of your life have you been trying to pound a square peg into a round hole? It usually feels something like exerting huge amounts of energy trying to accomplish something important and getting no measurable results. You may get some results but never seem to be able to break through to the greatness you seek.

Don't settle and be satisfied with where you are if you feel that you can accomplish much more. Find new ways to approach the issue. Try unorthodox, unusual methods to see if they will be more effective. Whatever you do, never stop trying to pursue your purpose.

Finding Purpose

Knowing your purpose is only the first step in a journey that will last a lifetime. It's not a straight path; it's a winding path. Defining and redefining your identity and your purpose are important keys to enjoying your purpose and making the best of this awesome gift.

Knowing your purpose is a gift. Many are offered it and turn it down. Others are like the child searching for Christmas gifts the week before Christmas. They think they've looked everywhere and still can't find it.

People get the idea that purpose is something grandiose and can only be lived out in large ways. While your overarching purpose and the fulfillment of it can be pretty amazing, it can also be lived daily in every area of life, big or small. It is a litmus test to help you determine what choices to make.

I recently heard an interview with Jeff Goins, author of *The Art of Work*. In the book, he talks about passion, purpose, and work. As I listened to the interview, I realized that many people think they should only be *working* in their area of passion and purpose. Instead, deploy your purpose and passion into every area of your life, including your work.

People often act and talk as if work is a bad thing. They can't wait for 5 o'clock, or for Friday, or for retirement. Life is too short to live in misery or dreading what we do. That doesn't necessarily mean quitting your job. It means having the ability to flourish wherever you are. It's a choice to flourish.

I know a school janitor who loves the kids at his school so much that he has decided to go to college to become a teacher, where he can have an even greater impact on their lives. He doesn't begrudge his time serving as their janitor, cleaning up their messes.

Instead, he relished in getting to know the kids and develop relationships. In a job where many would be miserable, he found purpose and passion. By identifying those things that bring you joy and bringing those things with you wherever you go, you help to fulfill your purpose in untold ways.

If you don't know where to start your search for purpose and passion, you're normal. It requires a new way of thinking. It's often outside your comfort zone where you find the best stuff in life, and this is no different. Your past experiences of feeling fulfilled and successful are clues—use them!

Before we define your purpose, let's explore your path and dig into a big bowl of spaghetti!

Spaghetti

Identifying and following your purpose usually doesn't look like a straight path, or even a gentle arc. It looks a lot more like a bowl of spaghetti. You don't know what twists and turns are going to happen before you set out on the journey. Many people see these twists and turns as a divergence from their purpose when it is merely a new twist on how or where they can *apply* their purpose. Celebrate when you find a new opportunity to explore or apply your purpose. It allows your purpose to grow and be enriched.

A good friend and I were discussing his recent retirement and exploring new purposes. He is a deeply analytical and wildly intelligent man whose opinion I value very highly. When I mentioned that I believe the pursuit of fulfilling our purposes looks more like a bowl of spaghetti than a straight path, he lit up.

He shares the belief that people often leave their purposeful pursuits because they don't see a clear, straight path. As a pastor who has done extensive mission work in Africa, he has a much clearer perspective on the differences between how we see purpose in our culture as opposed to other cultures. We seem to believe that we need to be able to see five, ten, and even twenty years into the future with perfect clarity to know that we are on the right path.

When our reality doesn't match what we envisioned, we assume that our vision was wrong. We assume there's a straight path, not a bowl full of twists and turns. It is the twists, turns, and even detours that cause us to be able to more deeply understand and develop our purpose, our calling. Welcome them.

The Calling

In my career, I've often said, "For some people, this is a job. For most, it's a career. For the blessed among us, it has become our calling." When you know you are actively pursuing your purpose, it feels much more like a calling. You know when it's right. At the office, I enjoy helping people be able to grow and accumulate their wealth in anticipation of creating a "work-optional" lifestyle. It's fun!

My real passion, though, is found in my definition of success with clients. Success to me is attending the funeral of the second one of them to die (assuming they are a couple) and being able to tell their beneficiaries two things: 1. They didn't run out of money; and 2. They had a lot of fun along the way! To me, fun means they are enjoying a purpose-filled life. I adore helping put together the puzzle pieces of their retirement journey and walking alongside them as they pursue their purpose.

How does that possibly align with my purpose? Simple. If I have helped them to create a traditional work-optional lifestyle and they choose to stay at the place they work for a lot longer, they are doing it because that's their choice. It's not required. They are pursuing their passion and purpose.

If they choose to leave that employer and retire, it gives us the opportunity to explore what their next mission will be in pursuing their purpose. Many times that means reigniting old passions they forgot they have and rediscovering their purpose. This fits perfectly into my personal purpose.

The Old Dog and the New Trick

Have you heard the expression that you can't teach an old dog new tricks? Well, it's crap. "Old dogs" *crave* new tricks. Regardless of age, people yearn to grow, develop, and explore. Too many have bought into the myth that after a certain age, you stop being capable of learning. As I've written this book over the last several months, much in the lives of the people I've written about has changed.

Remember the woman I mentioned who retired *from* something instead of *to* something and was living a lonely, purposeless, self-centered life? We had a wonderful discussion after she asked me where I get all of my energy. I said one word: *purpose*. I have a purpose for getting up in the morning that feeds my soul. I know why I'm here. It energizes me every day to do far more than anyone ever thought possible of me. It was then that she started the process of exploring the fact that she doesn't know her purpose. She is in the process of learning a new trick.

My friend may choose to explore her purpose further, and she may not. While you can teach an old dog new tricks, you can't force any dog to learn a trick. They must be willing. It's their choice. What choices have you made? Are you willing to learn a new trick? And remember, when it comes to learning and growing, age is irrelevant.

Investing in Yourself

Do you choose to make an intentional, well-planned investment in yourself? That's a powerful question. Let's break it down.

First, you have a choice. It is one of many and possibly the most important choice you will make. Investing in yourself is not always an easy project and not a commitment to be taken lightly. You need to be intentional about how you approach your investment. Intentionality means that it's not happenstance. You are making the most of who you are.

Your focus must be strong—zero in on developing your gifts and filling your toolbox with what you need to live your purpose and leave a powerful legacy in your wake. Stay tuned for a discussion of those needed tools for your toolbox in Part 3.

Second—remember the bowl of spaghetti? Though your purpose may lead you down various paths of opportunity, you need to stay with a well-planned path of personal growth and development. You may fill in some of the blanks differently because of your experiences, but you will stay committed to pursuing your purpose. The twists and turns and detours are in your path, not your commitment.

And finally: this is an investment. Investments don't always go up in value. While most of the time you will see yourself growing and developing, there will be tough times as well. You might realize along this path that you've made mistakes with friends and family in the past, mistakes you never knew about until now. Perhaps you learn that you were the root cause of some disaster and have to deal with that. You may find that you wronged someone and never knew it before.

The key with any investment in yourself is to find the lessons; find the opportunities instead of focusing on the obstacles. An investment in yourself will be the most valuable investment you ever make. You are worth it.

10. Solving the Mystery of Purpose

You've decided to make your greatest investment. You know that it's not a straight path. You are prepared to experiment and discover your purpose. Now to answer the question: What is my life purpose? You may have no idea. Or you may think you already know it, and you just want to make it SUPER. Either way, living a fulfilled life is closer than it's ever been.

The Mystery

Over the months of writing this book, I've had the opportunity to talk to many people about their purpose. For the most part, their reactions have surprised me. A very few people have a well-articulated purpose that really encompasses everything that I know to be true about them. Some have vague ideas of what it should be, either by their own definition or someone else's, but don't seem to have it fleshed out very well. Still others answer the question of purpose with vague looks, answers of "I don't know," and many times have tears in their eyes. We are wired for purpose—at some level, we all know this.

The mystery comes when we are trying to put our finger on exactly what our purpose could be.

- *What's my purpose?*

- *Why am I here?*

- *What is my contribution to the world?*

- *Do I have anything to offer that the world would want?*

- *How do I know that for sure?*

- *How can I choose one purpose in the vast sea of possibilities?*

- *What if my purpose doesn't coincide with what others believe my purpose should be?*

- *And what if I'm wrong?*

So much self-doubt. No wonder many people shy away from exploring their purpose and instead choose to go through the motions of life numbly, a slave to mediocrity.

Discovering your purpose in life is like solving a mystery. And just like a mystery, the first step is searching for clues. After that, you begin to put them together. Clues to your purpose are scattered throughout your past experiences. Some will likely be in your childhood and formative years. Others will be in your adult life.

For me, one of my most defining moments was my very first speech tournament at the age of 15. I was overly shy and completely petrified. I'd accidentally signed up for a speech class, not realizing that I would have to give speeches in front of people, both in class and at actual tournaments.

At the tournament, I read a simple poem and nearly cried each time I had to stand in front of people to be judged. I let myself relax after three rounds, thinking I was finished, until my coach told me I had to go to the fourth and final round since they'd given me good scores. In the finals, with the room filled with judges and fellow competitors, it took every ounce of strength for me to get the words out without crying. I stared at the paper, even though I had it memorized. Thankfully, it was a sad poem, so it looked like my downcast state was just a part of the performance. I won the tournament.

I learned at least two important lessons that day. First, I have a competitive streak and like winning (shy kids rarely win at anything, so this was new for me). Second, life is absolutely terrifying and yet *exhilarating* when you are operating outside your comfort zone.

Years later, partly because of this experience, my personal motto became, "The devil lives in your comfort zone and he likes it when you live there with him . . . so get out!" There are powerful clues to my purpose in this story, beyond those lessons I learned. Can you spot them? I'll give you a hint: I was my own first experiment.

Purpose Starts Internally

Purpose often starts by fulfilling it within ourselves. It evolves later to include others. My purpose includes helping people to reach for their *full potential*, and the first "people" I helped was me!

I had to realize that I was not living up to even a fraction of my potential and start down the road to doing so. I said *start* down that road. Remember, purpose is a journey. I've hit many twists and turns along the way. There have been many more of these defining moments over the years that have helped to shape, mold, and develop my purpose and my identity.

I still strive daily to live just outside my comfort zone, and I still work toward growing and improving myself. Writing this book is a perfect example. One of my fears—a carryover from the days when I was shy—is that people will judge my work poorly. I have a hard time with criticism when it's something into which I've poured myself. I feel like a fragile vase shattering whenever people criticize my work.

I know that this has held me back and will continue to do so if I let it. Therefore, I continue to work on maintaining my own Opportunity Mindset. The internal work will never stop, even when the rest of the world believes you have your act together and you are actively engaging your purpose for the benefit of others.

The First Exercise: The Tapestry of Your Purpose Begins

There are two exercises (in Chapters 10 and 12 respectively) to help you see the threads of your purpose and draw those threads together. You can find other exercises to help find your purpose online or in other books. The first exercise we will discuss is one I have found to be quite useful—I give much credit to Jeff Goins, author of *The Art of Work*, for helping me to articulate it.

List #1: Make a list of five past experiences that taught you *powerful lessons* about yourself. Sometimes we think of these as "pivot points," or defining moments, as my story above indicates. Perhaps these are times when you had a moment of maturity. Don't overthink this. Just quickly list out the five that come to mind first.

- Make a note of what lesson(s) you learned with each experience, and how they helped shape you. Take your time on this part.

List #2: Make a list of the five experiences that have given you the *greatest joy*. Again, no overthinking—just jot them down.

- Write down how each experience made you feel in just one or two words. Again, take your time.

For an example of what these lists can look like, I will provide Justine's answers to the above in Chapter 12.

Weaving the Tapestry: Forming Your Cape

What commonalities do you see between these experiences? There will be a thread or two between them that shows where you thrive. This is a guide to where you will find your purpose. Don't take shortcuts. Stop now and do this, even if you believe you already know your purpose.

You may be right on target already, but perhaps you still need to flesh it out a bit more. If nothing else, you will begin to get confirmation that you are on the right track. This may take you a while if you've never considered it before and have no idea what your purpose is. Remember to tell yourself that you are worth the effort.

✓ Check out the resources online at www.chooseyoursuperpower.com for the workbook to help guide you through this process.

Remember that your purpose should fill you until you are brimming with excitement, clarity, and peace. It's why you wake up in the morning. It will be a guiding force from which you operate. It serves as a framework through which you grow and develop.

Your purpose will be a litmus test through which you put all future opportunities and endeavors. If someone asks you to do something and it doesn't coincide with fulfilling your purpose, you may want to give additional consideration to whether or not it's appropriate to pursue.

11. Leading with Purpose

Who do you allow to define you? Who decides your significance and your purpose? The answer: *you* do. Our choices determine how the world views us and how we view ourselves.

Identity: The Cart Before the Horse

What is your identity? Is it tied to physical possessions or a particular person? Is it tied to your spouse, child, parent, friend, or coworker? Is it tied to an image you have created or are trying to create?

The norm for most people is to first create their identity, one in which they gain significance. Then that identity and significance determine what their purpose becomes. Their purpose follows from where they get their *feeling* of significance and ultimately from what their identity is tied to. In the long run, making personal progress and effective choices in this situation is like trying to push a rope when it should be *pulled*. The wrong part is leading.

Leading with your purpose allows you to make choices that feed into and fulfill your life. That purpose gives you significance. It helps to define your identity. From identity will flow the important goals, objectives, and even tasks that guide you on a daily basis. Do you see the difference between beginning with your purpose versus your identity? I will outline this formula soon—stay with me!

You are much more likely to feel fulfilled when your actions and activities are feeding into your higher purpose. You lay your head on the pillow at night knowing that you have made progress that means something. You sleep with a happy heart and wake with much more energy to make the next day just as brilliant as the last. Life becomes invigorating when your days are led with purpose—*your* purpose.

The truth is that, when asked about life purpose, I often see a blank stare or I am given an answer either about work (mostly from men) or about the kids (mostly from women). Try it yourself. Ask people you know, or ask strangers. The phrasing difference between the two questions listed below may completely change the answer.

1. What is your life purpose?

2. What is your current life purpose?

I discovered, in asking these questions, that simply adding the word "current" created a new answer for many of them. It went from "Raising my kids" to "Right now, it's raising my kids to be or do _____. I need to start thinking about what comes next." And just like that, with one extra word, my question has made them question their own purpose. Words have power. Even your choice of words has power.

Identity, Confidence, and Action

Is it really any wonder why our overall confidence and willingness to act on our decisions are often at very low levels? When we hit the "Why bother?" mentality and give in to circumstances—*reacting* instead of *acting*—our self-imposed identity and beliefs about ourselves say that we are quitters. From the perfectionist mentality to the why-bother mentality, what we lack is action. Decisive action creates confidence in making further progress.

As Michael Bernoff says so eloquently in his *Core Confidence* audio series, to build confidence requires that you make a decision, act on it, and follow through. Many people make decisions, and yet few act and follow through.

In a recent Q&A session with co-author of *The Confidence Code*, Claire Shipman, she said that to develop confidence we need to push just a little past our comfort zones and be brave. Bravery is a powerful thought. Bravery isn't taking a shower in the morning, having a cup of coffee, and getting in the car to head to work. That's normal.

Bravery is pushing past your norm, your comfort zone, and doing something that's unusual for you or doing it in an unusual way. It may mean getting up extra early to get in a good workout before work, skipping the coffee, or riding your bicycle to work. If this isn't your norm, it's at least a little brave.

Extreme bravery for you may be standing in front of a group of coworkers to make a presentation, singing in front of a crowd at karaoke night, or talking to a complete stranger. For some people, these are well within their comfort zone, and the actions they find extremely brave others find normal. Bravery is personal, as it should be.

Bravery—when combined with constant, incremental improvement—begets confidence. Imagine it. You step out of your comfort zone, not knowing what's about to happen. Will you succeed? Will it work? Or will you learn how to improve next time? Will you encourage others to step out of their comfort zones? So many thoughts running through your mind.

I once heard Brian Johnson, of *Optimal Living* fame, say that our subconscious mind is like a NASA supercomputer, while our conscious mind, by comparison, is like a Post-it note. Do your preparation, and let it rip. Have you done the work necessary to be successful? Have you prepared? If so, bravery is a little easier. In Brian's words, just let it rip! You won't just be *fine* for being brave. You'll be *better*. You realize the options aren't good or bad, success or failure. The only real options are *good, better, best*; or perhaps *win* or *learn*. Your mindset is in the right place.

Once you see that your worst-case imaginary outcomes never happened, you develop the confidence to move forward again. You really can do this. You can make a decision, act on it, and follow through with it. You not only survive it, you *thrive* on it.

Welcome to what the process of building your confidence feels like. And it all starts by making a choice, an intentional choice about pursuing your purpose.

Reframing Your Identity

You are redesigning and reframing your identity, one with your greater purpose in mind. It all starts with the decision to have a bias toward action. In this, being an *example* to others is much more valuable than being their instructor.

I occasionally have an opportunity to speak to groups of financial advisors. Since that first speech tournament, I don't usually have an issue speaking in front of groups. I was a competitive speaker in high school and college, taught in large university classrooms, and have spoken in many other settings as well. It's in my wheelhouse. Recently, excited that I would finally get to participate in a women's conference without having to speak, I turned in my RSVP.

A few weeks before the event, I received a request (since I was planning to be there anyway) wanting to know if I would be willing to speak at the event as an opener for the headliner. *What topic?* I asked. The answer came back that I could talk about whatever I wanted. *What is the headliner discussing?* Answer: "Not sure yet. You'll do great with whatever." Ugh. Not what I wanted to hear.

Let me tell you how incredibly intimidated I was at this point. Vickie, the headliner who everyone adored and was flown in from out of state, had been a personal inspiration to me for most of my career, even though I'd never met her. She was planning on attending the entire conference as well. That meant that this powerhouse woman was going to be sitting in the audience listening to my presentation.

It was nerve-racking for me to have little guidance on the topic and feel that she would be judging my every word. I prepared a presentation I thought might resonate with this group, prayed it wouldn't overlap her talking points, and just let my subconscious take over for me.

After the presentation was over, I had an opportunity to listen to her. She was as wonderful as I'd expected. I was quite surprised when she referenced my talk positively during *her* presentation. Afterward, several of the other women at the conference told me how well I'd done and that they were inspired to get out of their comfort zones and find ways to expand their horizons.

I've been in touch with many of them since and they have done just that. I had an opportunity to demonstrate what it looks like to step out, and they followed my lead. I can *tell* them how important it is to be brave, but it's best done when I show it myself. It had the nice side effect of making me more bold as well. Vickie and I now have a good relationship and speak frequently.

12. Thriving with Purpose

You shape and mold your own identity. You choose it, just like you choose your purpose. With purpose, and your identity firmly grounded *within* your purpose, you begin to thrive.

You've worked through the first exercise and begun to see a few of the threads that make your purpose and make it unique to you. Let's keep going.

We now know that it all starts with your purpose, and purpose is like a tapestry that is woven and enriched over time. We are just beginning to find the common threads and will continue here with a legacy exercise. Some call this the "eulogy test." People have used it for years to pretend people will say kind words about them when they are gone. But it's far more important than that. When done well, it points to the purpose that defines your identity and significance.

What do you choose to set as your life's purpose? It's okay to have more than one purpose in life, or even one over-arching purpose and several "missions" within it. From there you can work through your significance and identity.

I've heard several ways to help determine purpose, significance, and—ultimately—to shape your identity. Though it seems a little morbid at first, I've found the following to be quite useful—and I've added a little twist at the end. Complete the following exercise and you will be closer to honing in on that over-arching purpose.

Complete the sentences on the next page. You may revise them later.

My life's purpose is to: _____
_____

At my funeral (hopefully many years into the future), I would hope that people from various areas of my life say this about me:

Family:
_____
_____

Co-workers:
_____
_____

Friends:
_____
_____

Neighbors:
_____
_____

My Community:
_____
_____

As your friends and family finish speaking about you, the pastor asks if there is anyone else who would like to speak. Much to everyone's surprise, several hands are raised. You didn't really know these people. You met them briefly, yet you made a powerful impression. What do they say?

"Strangers" whom I impacted:

_____

_____

These comments help you see how you wish to be remembered—your legacy. There may be several that are the same, or all are the same, or each may be different. Take your time now to imagine each in the greatest detail possible. You may even want to split out family members and friends into different, more specific, groups.

Be specific and vivid. This is important. It is from these that you begin to see what your ultimate, over-arching choice is for your life purpose. We discuss more of this in the Skyscrapers section, where it all comes together. It's important that the process start with purpose.

What common threads do you see in the answers above? Combine these with the answers from the previous exercise and the lists you created. You should start to see some commonalities. It is these common threads that will weave together to illuminate your purpose.

Justine's Purpose

Justine, a student of this process who recently walked through the exercises with me, was desperate to find her purpose. She was feeling directionless. Here are a few notes from the exercises we've covered as she went through them.

The Lists:

- Powerful Experiences:

    - *Had kids very young (teen mother)—made her stronger; resiliency*

    - *Earned a spot to go to Vegas at a previous employer—realized she can do anything she puts her mind to*

    - *Competition team travelled overseas—broadens horizons; likes to be part of a winning team*

    - *Coming to current employer—out of her comfort zone; willing to take on challenge of no experience*

- Pure Joy Experiences:

    o *Watching her sons finish school—she overcame circumstances and passed that on to her sons*

    o *Her father wanted to take a trip to Germany and she was able to take him—selflessly giving to her father who had done so much for her*

    o *Took her husband to Scotland—new experience and she'd never been out of the US before; amazing growth of perspective*

Legacy Test: What do the following people say about you at your funeral?

- *Family: "Always took time for me, giving woman with a great heart"*

- *Friends: The same as above, plus that she helped teenage girls through a non-profit; genuine mentorship to the girls; always took the time for people with a warm smile and caring hugs*

- *Co-Workers/Clients: "Treated us (clients) like her best friends; serious and focused on excellence with us (co-workers)" o Neighbors: (she had just moved and wasn't sure how to answer yet)*

- *Community: From the Chamber to her Optimist Club to the community overall (since she will be mayor), "She's awesome!"*

- *Strangers: "She took time for people, no matter who they were; she inspired us to do more."*

Common Threads:

- Servant heart

- Lifting others up; empowering

- Likes competing

- Overcoming adversity and sharing the path to success

Significance

Once you've identified your life's purpose and ultimately looked at how it applies in each area of your life, begin the process of sorting through how to make this impact with intentionality. Think of your possibilities as the open road. You can go nearly anywhere.

Your life's purpose is not your destination, but the entire journey. The goals you set continue to serve as waypoints to indicate whether you are going in the right direction. Your SIGNIFICANCE then flows from the progress you make in moving in the direction of your purpose.

When you receive positive feedback consistent with the direction in which you are going, you know that you've come closer to living your life's purpose. Sometimes achieving goals brings external recognition. Sometimes it's purely internal. Either way, there is value in making sure that you acknowledge the significance of what you've accomplished. It reinforces that you're on the right path.

Let's look at this traveling analogy for a moment. Let's simplify purpose and assume that your life purpose is to travel the world. Your waypoints are goals to ensure that you're moving, hopefully in the right direction. If your purpose is to see the world and you never leave Kansas, are you living your purpose? If all you do is go back and forth between Kansas and Missouri, is that living your purpose of seeing the world?

Sounds silly, doesn't it? How many times do you keep doing what you've been doing because that's the way you've always done it? Inaction is a choice. It makes it very unlikely that you are moving in your desired direction. Your feeling of significance, gained through accomplishing goals, helps make sure you are actually seeing the world.

Identity

Your IDENTITY then is the vehicle you drive. No, I did not just say that the vehicle you drive defines you. It's just an analogy. What will get you to *who* and *where* you need to be? To see the world, do you need to be flashy and exciting? Do you need to take a lot with you, need a van or an RV?

What about fuel efficiency? Do you want to have to stop frequently to refill your fuel tank? Some identities require more recharging than others. Some can go on for extreme distances without needing to stop to refuel or for maintenance.

My husband describes himself as highly fuel-efficient. He likes to conserve his energy. This is typical considering his love of Gracie Jiu-Jitsu, which he teaches daily. In fact, you can see a lot of his purpose mirrored in the Gracie Way. It's a martial art designed for the smaller person to defeat the bigger, stronger, heavier opponent. This requires allowing others to burn energy while conserving your own energy.

It doesn't mean that he uses minimal effort or doesn't set and achieve goals. In fact, it's quite the opposite. He targets his effort in very refined ways toward a very specific purpose. He is highly efficient and wastes very little time on things that don't obviously serve his purpose. He is an adventure bike—highly focused, extremely efficient, and adaptable to nearly any situation.

In this analogy, how would you define your vehicle? If we want to see the world, how many miles will you go? Will you need to change vehicles? Absolutely! Friends, this continent is not the entire world. You may need, at times, to be on a boat or in an airplane. You may need to walk or run or swim or fly or climb, and occasionally let others whom you trust take the wheel.

You will change, grow, and develop over the journey as the terrain and circumstances change. That's okay. As long as you continue to live your purpose and reach the waypoints, your identity can flex without breaking who you are at heart.

This is very different from how it works if you put your identity in front of your purpose, which many people do. With identity leading, you easily take offense if you think anyone has challenged that identity or circumstances no longer support it. You feel dejected and overwhelmed or you feel like a victim. Neither one helps you pursue your purpose. Neither allows for you to become a Super-*anything*.

If you want your purpose to become a Super Power, thrive by leading with purpose.

Identity, Actions, Feelings

Once you have zeroed in on your identity and have a solid, well-defined purpose, overcoming the challenges ahead becomes far simpler. Your normal tendency, as articulated by several different authors and speakers, is to let your feelings determine your actions. Then those actions determine your identity.

For example, if I don't feel like waking up in the morning, I hit my snooze button—my action, or rather *in*action—until there is no time to spare and I have no choice but to get out of bed. At that point, I grudgingly stand up and go through the motions of getting ready for the day. I am not a morning person. When I did not *feel* like waking up in the morning, my actions reinforced that feeling. Then I let my inability to start my day with vigor define my identity as a non-morning person. This is how it looks for most people today.

Feelings → Actions → Identity → Significance → Purpose (or Lack of Purpose)

This happens every day in houses around the world. In fact, until recently, that was me. I didn't realize how much I felt like a failure until I started leading myself in the opposite direction. Hitting the snooze button repeatedly is like starting your day by saying, "I'm off to a crappy start and don't even have the willpower to wake up when I need to!"

Purpose → Significance → Identity → Actions → Feelings

Now let's look at it from the opposite perspective. Once I have a purpose that excites me into getting started with my day, I wake up almost two hours earlier every day. I don't sleep until the last minute and I rarely hit the snooze button (never say never).

My day starts with a feeling of accomplishment—in fact, much of my best work and thinking happens before anyone else in the house is active. After a start like that, how can I *not* rock my day?

This can be applied, in Brian-Tracy fashion, to the biggest, hardest challenge you have in your day. If you wait until later when you *feel* ready to tackle it, you will spend the day in unproductive dread of doing the task.

If you put it off until tomorrow or next week or next month, your inaction compounds the stress and perceived difficulty. You are far less able to accomplish your goals and fulfill your purpose. In fact, having the order of IDENTITY to ACTIONS to FEELINGS *backward* is common in self-described procrastinators. I used to be one of those, too. Get this straight and you will find liberation, freedom like you never thought possible.

13. Build Your Skyscraper

Tall buildings, such as skyscrapers, have deep foundations. Why? Because it's wasteful to spend all of that money to build if it is going to come crashing down and become a pile of rubble! Think of it like an iceberg. Which was stronger: the *Titanic* or the iceberg?

Superheroes have strong foundations, as we discussed in the Autonomy section. They have a moral compass that allows them to build incredible legacies. Their deep foundations allow them to live in the world without being forced into worldly norms.

You have foundations too, and like a skyscraper or an iceberg, there's often far more below the surface that holds you steady than anyone might imagine. Like many important areas in your life, most people fail to realize they have a choice in this arena: shallow or deep foundations. Let's take a moment and unpack this analogy.

If you want to build a one-or two-story home, what foundational options will a builder usually give you? That's right—slab, crawl space, or basement. What are the benefits? A slab is an inexpensive foundation made of concrete, which is pretty stable and quite able to sustain the "load," or weight, of the structure you want to build. In a home with a crawl space, the contractor digs something called "footings." These are concrete pillars on which the house is built and are also fairly inexpensive compared to the cost of a basement. That final option, basement, is much more expensive to build. But people like the extra space and it provides added safety in a tornado (I'm from Kansas . . . we think about these things).

If you want to build a *very* tall building, especially a skyscraper, you need very deep footings or foundations. It takes a tremendous subterranean structure to support both the height and the weight of a massive building. What happens if you build a very tall building on a slab foundation? When faced with a stiff wind or mild tremors or even a normal settling of the ground, it starts to falter.

What kind of person are you? Do you have shallow foundations, and perhaps want to deepen them? Are your foundations already deep and wide? What type of life do you wish to lead? I must admit that one of my life's greatest, repeated disappointments is witnessing wasted potential.

People, like buildings, must have foundations. The difference between you and buildings is that you can continue to dig and improve your foundations even after you've built some of your structure. It's called self-development. These foundations are deepened by improving your fundamentals and growing your skill-sets and mindsets.

"Slab" people will not be able to safely build very high before they encounter problems. These are usually the people who believe that "good" is good *enough*. Sometimes, what they view as good is not what most people would consider good. The term "good" is very subjective.

How do you identify a "slab" person? They only speak of shallow things, rarely more than small talk. They tend to be virtually obsessed with social media, traditional media, and other external sources. They crave external stimulation on a consistent basis. They tend to spend/waste time and energy instead of investing time and energy in self-development, helping others, and pursuing their passions and purpose.

Look around you. Do you see the people who sit in the restaurant with their family staring at their phones instead of interacting? (This is called the iPhone Effect.) Are you aware how many people are more informed about the latest happenings of the Kardashians or spend their time obsessed with the outcome of this week's episode of *Survivor*?

Please, don't misunderstand. We all have "slab" moments. But you are likely reading this because you don't want to unpack your things and *live* a "slab" life. Otherwise, you wouldn't be looking to improve yourself at all. You wouldn't be on a quest to find your purpose.

Being a "slab" person is a choice, even if it happens by default. There is nothing wrong with people who make this choice. Though it tends to be self-limiting, it is their choice. Not mine. They don't typically hurt others with their "slab" lifestyle. In fact, many are very nice people. People are given the gift of free will. You can choose to change and grow, or you can choose not to. What a gift!

It's when people with a slab (or even a basement foundation) attempt to build a skyscraper that problems arise. They failed to build the foundation deep enough to sustain the height and weight of their lives. When adversity hits, life begins to crumble. These folks can be quite dangerous to those around them. For example, the majestic towers of wealth and prowess built by people like Bernie Madoff came crumbling down around him and all those in his world when his Ponzi scheme came to light. The Wall Street traders who were "smarter" than the rest of us and gambled their way into what became the 2008 financial crisis built their skyscrapers on shallow foundations.

They didn't have the ethical foundations needed to build very high. It has happened over and over in the course of history—even modern history. Tall towers built on slab foundations are destined to fall.

"Though the rain comes in torrents and the floodwaters rise and the winds beat against that house, it won't collapse because it is built on bedrock." (Matthew 7:25) In this parable, Jesus talks about building a house on bedrock (following Christ's teaching) as strong. A house built on sand (not following His teaching) "will collapse with a mighty crash." (Matthew 7:27)

Foundations Are Fundamentals: What Do You Need to Improve in Order to Grow?

You are ready to build your skyscraper. What is your skyscraper? What future, legacy, or amazing creation do you want to craft? How does it look? Imagine it clearly. What do you need to choose to do to make sure you have the right foundation? What are your fundamentals to make sure you build it well?

For me, my skyscraper is the legacy I wish to leave to my family, friends, and the world. It is tall and wide. It has a cross and a steeple at the top pointing its magnificence to the heavens where all of the credit truly belongs. It includes a library of books with great ideas on how to move your life forward and constantly grow.

It has a place for people to grow and create and another to just be still and *be*. There are many rooms to represent facets of my personality and purpose, many rooms to serve others, many where people can go to explore. There are whole floors dedicated to the people who I have helped along the way to build their skyscrapers. The walls of those floors are adorned with pictures of their skyscrapers, many much taller and wider and grander than my own. This makes me smile.

Your skyscraper is your purpose, your legacy. In this final exercise, envision the size of your skyscraper, its floors and rooms. What happens within those walls? What adorns the walls? Use what you learned in the previous exercises. Like an architect, envision your skyscraper in final form. Write it. Draw it. Plan it. From there, you can start digging the foundations that will make your purpose possible and your legacy last.

To build my skyscraper, I must work hard at many fundamentals. I am a mother, a wife, a teacher, a coach, a writer, a financial advisor, and an occasional motivator. I have many roles and wear many hats. To work my fundamentals to build this grand tower, I first have to start by making sure that I am okay with who I am and find and develop my strengths.

I need to find the commonalities between my various roles— and there are common threads. For starters, these are generally other-centric. Focusing outside of oneself extensively consumes tremendous amounts of energy. Knowing that time and energy are both limited resources, I must use both wisely and in meaningful ways. Time can be used to gain energy through exercise.

For example, getting exercise is foundational for me. If I don't get adequate exercise, my energy levels fall and I am less able to maintain momentum toward pursuing my purpose. My eating habits become worse, and that makes me even less likely to get the exercise my body needs.

It's a vicious cycle that I must intentionally break or I waste both my time and my energy. Therefore, maintaining an exercise routine is a key fundamental to building my deep foundation.

There are more. This is merely one example. Know your fundamentals and understand that it's okay to change them as you grow. It's like digging through dirt and sand until you hit bedrock.

The deeper you go, the more likely you'll need to change your tools and approach. It's a great sign. You're making progress.

Take the time to identify your strengths first. Can you leverage these strengths to help build your foundation and a taller skyscraper? Do you need to expand your skill-set? Enhance your mindset? Are you sure that skyscraper you envisioned is big enough? Could it be more? Are you willing to dig those foundations just a little deeper?

I'm sure that as you consider the people you know that you will recognize some who have created excellent skyscrapers with deep, solid foundations. Surround yourself with as many of these people as you can. Ask them questions so you can learn what fundamentals they have developed into their standard practices.

- Are they early risers?

- Do they engage in purposeful silence or prayer daily?

- How important is exercise in their lives?

- Do they routinely practice visualization?

- What have they chosen to do to either minimize the effects of weaknesses or transform them into strengths?

- When they feel out of balance, how do they regain that equanimity?

You will find the answers to these questions fascinating. Today I asked a new friend about his fundamentals. He said that he spends the very first part of his day jotting down ten things he is grateful for in his life and the world. What a great way to start your day!

Your skyscraper—your purpose—much like the life of a Superhero, can lift up and inspire others. You can carry them to greater heights alongside you. To do this, you cannot settle for living a mediocre, shallow life. You must reach for far more.

If you choose to strive for *great* instead of settling for "good enough," I would encourage you to write out your life purpose. Many people develop more than one. While you should understand that it may change over time, it begins to show you what your skyscraper can look like. It points you to what foundations—both type and depth—you will need.

Many people struggle with the concept of defining life purpose. I thought it suitable to share mine now.

> *My life purpose is to INSPIRE and ENCOURAGE people to BE and DO far more than they ever thought possible—to harness their PASSIONS and reach for their FULL POTENTIAL.*

Take a few minutes—close your eyes if necessary—and begin the journey of intentionally looking for your life purpose. Visualize your skyscraper. Complete or review the previous exercises about how you want to be remembered. You may not be able to see much more than the first few floors of your skyscraper right now. That's okay. Have faith that as you move in the direction of your purpose more will become clear. Look to the foundations you need in order to build higher. Then start digging. We are approaching Mastery.

Mastery is digging deeply, improving skills, deepening foundations. In the next section, you will explore how to dig those deep foundations so you can reach greater heights with your purpose. You will encounter obstacles. It's normal. The Superhero life means that you have to blast through the obstacles and find opportunity. That journey begins now. Are you ready?

PART 3

Mastery

Supers must live *in* the world but not be *of* the world. In Part 1: Autonomy, it was clear that to move from human to superhuman you must live by your own moral compass, not by the same porous standards of others. Living by a firmly entrenched set of morals will build in you stronger empathy. You will find that your level of empathy, though often painful, is important to your journey. It keeps you human.

As you move through Part 3, on Mastery of your Purpose, you will realize how a Super Purpose can become a Super Power. This invigorating process, rife with potential pitfalls, is much like those faced by Superheroes in the stories. You will dig deep to build the foundations, the fundamentals, needed to reach Super-status. Begin by taking a fresh look at what you think you already know.

14. Be Completely Out of Your Mind!

I would encourage you to live a life mostly out of your mind.

Let me explain. Instead of viewing everything through the lens of how it affects you, consider putting yourself in the place of others. View the world and situations from their perspectives. This is not an easy task if you've never tried it. Start small.

Drive or walk up to the front of your house and pretend that you've never seen it before. How does it look? Be specific to document what you notice.

- Is the lawn in good shape? Or is it obvious your pet has been let out frequently to use it as a litter box?

- Is your front door inviting? Is it easy to walk up the front steps or are there barriers—both physical and psychological—to people who may be coming over as guests? Does the doorbell work? Or is your house the picture of manicured perfection?

- Assume this were a new friend's house and you were going there for the first time. How would you feel?

The point of this exercise isn't to point out the flaws in your house or apartment. Nor is it to make you feel that you're better than others because you put a high price on keeping it nice. Choose to see the world through the eyes of others, to see from their perspective. This is how we gain insight.

As an example, let's take a visit to my house. My husband says I'm a little OCD. I beg to differ, as you will see. First, in order for people to find our house, I must give very detailed instructions. Once you finally get to the house, you are greeted with tall grass, flowerbeds full of weeds, playgrounds in both the front and back yards, and countless bikes and kid's toys littering the yard. In order to keep my sanity, I have to close my eyes to much of this chaos (at least for now).

Knowing it's chaos, how can I let it stay that way for long? Simple. I have to make choices. I simply cannot handle two jobs, two kids, writing, very little free time during daylight hours, and the normal to-do list every mother and wife seems to have. Would I like it to be blissfully beautiful outside? Of course! But I don't have enough time or help getting and keeping it done.

When you approach someone else's house—like mine—stop for a minute before passing judgment and be open to the possibility that they may have made the choice to prioritize differently than you have. Or perhaps they have a different skill-set and don't know how to handle areas that you find commonplace and simple. (For the record, I am well aware of how to garden and maintain the outside of the house.)

The Eyes Have It

That brings us to the next step: viewing situations through other people's eyes. How do they view you and the choices you've made? There are many lessons in that one question. The biggest lesson is discovering what falls into the blind-spot of your comfort zone.

You get cozy in your own comfort zone while you develop a blind-spot that often results in passing judgments on the choices of others and condemning them without understanding their perspective. This is divisive, harms everyone, and helps no one. This is a prevalent problem in today's society.

So get out of your mind—and into someone else's. I am neither condemning nor commending choices made by others. I am merely saying that before you decide how to respond to it, look at it from a different perspective. In today's society, we tend to make others into bad guys, or villains, when they simply see the world through different lenses.

Denise, a friend, was over at my house recently. She works as a laborer at a company that recently had three rounds of layoffs. She survived all of them, but she is very bitter toward the company. However, she's not looking to change employers, since she is "just a laborer" (her words, not mine).

She knows that I often have a different take on life and wanted to know if all businesses are in business just to make money and don't care about the employees. I grew up in an entrepreneurial family with parents who owned a plumbing, heating, and air-conditioning business. I also work professionally with business owners and executives of all sizes and flavors. I wasn't sure she knew this, so I shared my background with her.

After telling her that most of the business owners and executives I had met over the years are very protective of their employees and really want to serve their customers and provide good jobs to their employees, she looked confused.

"I've never heard anything like that before," she said. She grew up in a family of laborers.

I asked her if I could explain to her why a company may have a layoff.

"Let's assume for a moment that you're a diabetic. Your body's systems are in chaos and situations beyond your control cause your blood sugar to be out of control for too long. The doctor sits you down and gives you your options. He either amputates your leg or you will die. What do you choose?"

Without hesitating, she chose amputation.

I looked at her and said, "Welcome to a layoff. You don't want to lose the leg any more than a company wants to lose a valuable piece of itself—its valued employees. Would you rather the company die—go bankrupt—and all jobs be lost, or choose to lay people off until they can turn the company around?"

Denise had never even considered what it might be like from the company's point of view. She had no idea that the people having to make that decision and deliver the news of a layoff might be very pained by it. That's when she started opening up to the idea of viewing the world through different eyes.

How can you apply this in your life? Before you get upset about the impact someone else's choice has on you, stop for a moment to consider it from their perspective. Choose to respond, not merely to react.

- Do they really feel that they have a choice?

- Are they aware of all the options they have, or do you see more options that they don't see?

- If so, could you share those options with them?

- What would you do in their situation with the choices they have available?

Doing this requires that you get completely out of your mind, at least occasionally, and into someone else's. I find it helpful to make it a habit on a daily basis to find one other person and view the world through their eyes. Not only will it help you to understand them better, it will also help *you* see more choices and options. If nothing else, it should help you realize why none of the neighbors ever approach your house!

The Myth of Perfection

Perfection is a beautiful thing. Have you ever thought of or dreamed about having something perfect? Would you like to maintain the perfect balance in life? How about finding the perfect hairstyle? Or the perfect life partner? Or perfectly well-behaved children? Or maybe you dream of being perfect yourself.

Achieving perfection is a myth. And that's okay. We don't need to be perfect. We only need to be aware that neither we, nor any aspect of our lives, will achieve and maintain this lofty status.

As long as we are focused on growing and developing and improving, we can enjoy the journey.

So if the journey isn't about reaching perfection, where are we headed?

Strive for Excellence, Not Perfection

Operating under the illusion that perfection is attainable is counter-productive and discouraging. That idyllic life—though you may have a few days like that—will not hold for the long term. Those days are likely an illusion themselves. And when they fade, we get discouraged.

There are two enemies at work here. First, the *discouragement* of not being perfect robs you of the joy you can have in developing yourself, and you quit. "Other people seem to have it figured out, so what's wrong with me?" That's a flawed comparison. They don't have it "figured out" any more than you do. They are also striving for excellence and may be ahead of you on the path. They are not perfect. Learn from them and you may be able to avoid a few of the pitfalls.

Second, you become *complacent* when you set your sights too low and think you've reached the pinnacle of your potential—when it is in fact the plateau. As Jim Collins would say, "Good is the enemy of great." I would like to add to that by saying: Good enough is also the enemy of improvement. When you feel that your situation is good enough, you stop caring about improvement.

Sadly, the first enemy often leads to the second. You get discouraged by not being able to attain or sustain your vision of perfection, and so you choose to settle for less, for good enough.

This choice is made in many areas of life. Deciding to focus more intensely on creating improvement in one area of life while letting the others remain fairly stagnant for a time is not the danger.

The biggest danger is when we accept complacency in *all* areas of life. You unwittingly make the choice to become numb. That numbness in one area bleeds into other areas of your life. You don't get the promotion you feel you deserve at work, even though you worked very hard to get it. You stop trying to improve your skill-set.

Don't believe the myth of perfection. That's all it is—a myth. All it does is lead people to inaction.

An example of this phenomenon can be found in the book *The Confidence Code*, in which studies show that women want to be 100% qualified for a job before they will even consider applying for it. Men, on the other hand, will pursue that same opportunity when they feel they have only 60% of the qualifications required. They assume they will figure the rest out on the job. And guess what? The men are right! They tend to be less hampered by the myth of perfection, in this area at least. This myth has held women back from pursuing leadership roles for years. As the authors, Katty Kay and Claire Shipman, said, "Women are conditioned to be perfect. Men are conditioned to be brave."

Generalities aside, subscribing to the myth of perfection is common for all people—especially those who have low confidence levels. So, regardless of your gender, strive to be brave and cast aside the myth of perfection.

The Antidote to the Myth of Perfection: Constant Improvement

For many of the people I have coached, the most effective approach has been to focus on developing processes for constant incremental improvements. Focusing on solid, purposeful processes helps keep the discouragement at bay.

Constant, incremental improvements help you recognize small improvements that compound to be much greater results in the future. These small improvements lead to increased confidence. Speakers and authors, from Jim Rohn to Tony

Robbins and countless others, have preached this for years. Why? It works!

If you have a desired outcome that you'd like to achieve in one year or five years or over your lifetime, it can become overwhelming. The key is to develop a simple process designed to reach your outcome. Then focus on working that process.

You must not be married to the process. Only "date" the process. If it's not working in any way, analyze why it's not working and make a course correction. Don't be too quick to throw out the process. Just be willing to objectively analyze and see if it's an issue of needing more time for it to work or if you need to change some component.

Let's say that you want to write a book. The average book usually has between 200–300 pages, more in some genres. That's a lot of pages to fill with words. In fact, when I started writing, I was told the average page contains 400 words. That means that you need to write approximately 100,000 words. Sound overwhelming? Though many people want to write a book, most people don't write it because the task seems so daunting.

Take that 100,000-word novel and break it down into 500 words per day (which is what I set as a goal when writing this book). That's 200 days. If you can do that five days a week for 40 weeks, you have 100,000 words on paper. The process is to write 500 words per day, knowing that in approximately 9–10 months you will have written your book.

I spent nearly 20 years not writing because, even though I had several book outlines, I hadn't thought to break it down into manageable pieces in this way. I hadn't made it a process. It was easy to make excuses for why I couldn't write. After all, how on earth can I do that while running one business full time, helping my husband run another, coaching and training other financial advisors, and taking care of two small children (currently ages 8 and 2)? It seemed pure lunacy.

That's when I combined the process with the concept of making small, incremental improvements so that I could see progress. I started tracking the number of words each day as well as the accumulation in what I call my writer's log. It was fun to see the number of words growing, and I felt that I was making progress daily, bit by bit. I even decided that it was so much fun that I'd "show up" to write on the weekends as well.

This could easily be applied to many other goals as well: healthy eating, fitness, responsible spending, time-blocking, saving and investing, organizing, and nearly any other area that is important to you. By combining the meaningful process to the constant, incremental improvements, you can continually stay on the path to creating a more fulfilling and optimal life. And it can actually be quite fun!

Procrastinators Beware

The ultimate downfall of the perfectionist is procrastination. It is much like the question of the chicken and the egg: *Which came first*? Were you a perfectionist or a procrastinator?

Wanting everything to be just right, over-preparing, over-analyzing, and over-thinking—common threads among perfectionists—often lead to procrastination. Or were you a procrastinator who didn't "feel" like doing anything so you put it off under the guise of being a perfectionist?

It's a vicious cycle: "I can't act yet because I need to make sure it's right first." . . . "It's not right enough so I need to wait until I have the drive, motivation, inspiration, whatever to work on it." . . . "I haven't had a chance to work on it enough so I still can't do it. I need more time." Sound familiar? If so, you're not alone.

Procrastinators use perfection as their excuse. You say you are a perfectionist when the truth is that it gives you a lovely excuse never to finish, and in many cases never to actually start at all. Procrastinators believe it takes away the sting of the myth of perfectionism, but they couldn't be farther from the truth. Stop deceiving yourself. After all, being a perfectionist or a procrastinator is a choice.

15. Change Your Thinking and Rule Your World

What motivates you? Is it something big and grand like changing the world, helping people, creating a new life saving technology? Or is it something more immediate and tangible like a day out with friends, money, or more time to focus on your passions?

For most, it is some of both. You have grand aspirations and goals. These are things you'd like to accomplish in your lifetime. I started my career wanting to help 1,000 households to and through retirement and put at least 500 kids through college by doing financial advising with families. A doctor friend wanted to help her patients have successful pregnancies and deliver healthy babies. Another friend wants to raise four healthy, well-adjusted children who follow Christ and help others to seek Him also. These are lofty, long-term goals, and they feed our souls. It speaks to our passions. That's good.

So why is it so hard to stay on track to accomplish these?

1. First, while motivating, they are almost overwhelming if not broken down into bite-sized pieces. It's the old

concept of eating the elephant one bite at a time. The size of your goals overwhelms you and it becomes hard to see where exactly to start.

2. Second, inertia is a powerful force to overcome. Regardless of whether you are "wired" for productivity or not, getting and staying motivated is challenging when you're in a slump. It can take a long time to see results. In some ways, this is discouraging. How long does it take to work with 1,000 households all the way through their retirement years? It can't be measured in years. It must be measured in *decades*. So how can a person feel motivated on a daily basis when the motivations are so long term?

3. Finally, people are—as Stephen Covey articulated so brilliantly—often ruled by the urgent, not the important. Pursuing lives with purpose is extremely important. The emergencies that arise can frequently make you feel like your pursuit of purpose has been derailed. *You* are in charge of pursuing your purpose. *You* can continue to pursue it despite the urgencies that often arise.

Each time that I feel interrupted in pursuit of my purpose, I stop and put the current interruption through my own litmus test. I can usually find a way to utilize it to move my purpose forward. It's all in how I choose to perceive the interruption. I'm not perfect—remember, perfection is a myth—and it often takes me some frustration before I remember to engage the "purpose filter." I'm working on shortening the time it takes me to remember to use that filter. How?

By focusing on partnering your long-term motivations, motives, and goals with short-term motivations, motives, and goals. This can drive you in the direction of the long-term. The simple answer is that, as long as they are in alignment, it's best to have both short-and long-term goals as well as small and large motivators. They are not mutually exclusive; in fact, combining the two can lead to tremendous momentum that even *exceeds* your goals.

Perhaps an example would help. Working with my goals and motivations as outlined above, I want to help 1,000 households to and through retirement, as well as help to put at least 500 kids through college. I won't be able to do it all at once. I have to take it one family at a time, one conversation at a time. That's a start. Work with one family in a comprehensive manner, then move to work with the next. I can reward myself with something that motivates me today toward wanting and desiring to meet and engage that next family.

I like chocolate. I rewarded myself years ago with chocolate, and lots of it! At the time, weight loss was the last thing I needed to worry about since I'd lost 20 pounds after starting in a new career. For every five people with whom I had a meaningful conversation and moved our relationship forward, I earned a Hershey's Kiss. Yum! After a few months, my desk contained a massive pile of earned and uneaten Kisses. I got so excited about all of the people I was helping that I got enough satisfaction from the relationships and no longer needed the chocolate (at least as a motivator . . . we all still need chocolate).

Sidenote: Putting yourself out in front of people who will often reject you, your efforts, and your work can be extremely demotivating. If you live in that sort of world (and many of us who are pursuing our purpose do), you will need small motivations to help overcome rejection, learn from it, and move on. As a new financial advisor, countless people slammed the door in my face, hung up on me, yelled at me, and even took my advice and followed it with someone else.

*Rejection is extremely hard on the psyche. I constantly reminded myself of the truth: Nothing in life worth having is easy. **If your pursuits are easy, they're probably not worth very much.** Now I am blessed to work with a group of amazing people. They are far more than clients. They are friends, and we are on this fantastic journey through the rest of their lives together. The early rejection was worth it. The jerks weeded themselves out.*

After a while, it became an endless sea of people and an overwhelming number of relationships to manage. That's when I was asked to help train other financial advisors to work at a higher level with their clients. This was a huge opportunity to fast-track my goal and was extremely motivating! I could reach *exponentially* more people. Wow! What a great chance to leverage what I'd started. Through this outreach, I've had an opportunity to extend and exceed my original motivation, philosophy, and reach.

In writing this book, I have found the opportunity to increase that potential even more, and my next books will do that even further. My next book focuses on people who want to continue to pursue their full purpose and potential through the traditional retirement years. The third book will focus on the younger, millennial generation, defining, designing, and deploying their life purpose. Talk about super-charging your Super Power!!!

You may be highly motivated and still can't seem to break through to the greater levels of achievement that you know are possible. You feel like you are running at full speed and getting nowhere. Or perhaps you feel like you're banging your head on a glass wall. Pursuing your purpose is on the other side—and you can see it so clearly—you just don't know how to get through. Is that you? If so, the next section is just for you!

Chef vs. Cook

You are taught to follow the rules. In school, you are to sit down, pay attention, take notes, study hard, ask for help if you need it, and—most importantly—follow directions. We teach our children to do much the same at home and reward them by not putting them on Ritalin and giving them privileges and trinkets. In the workplace, you work hard to reach a level of success determined by the company's bottom-line goals in your attempt to gain recognition and advancement within the company.

The Recipe

This recipe you learn from a young age helps you succeed . . . to a point. After years of "following the recipe," you may hear or read something that makes you wonder what's really possible. At some level, you realize that you have become a cook.

Many employers who have world-class training programs, like my company, do an amazing job

of streamlining the process and getting people to successful levels more quickly and consistently. They do that by teaching people to follow the recipe. That works well in helping people who are previously untrained in a certain area to be knowledgeable, competent, and successful. Our world-class training departments are great at creating cooks, following a proven recipe. My company is not alone in this.

The world, and many employers, are very good at teaching people to be cooks. You are very good at following the recipe, which is often someone else's recipe. When you feel like you are running in place or banging your head against that glass wall trying to get to the other side, that means you've become a really good cook and it's time to step up your game.

You need to change your approach. What got you this far will not take you where you want to be. To get through to the other side of the glass and to get traction in your pursuit of your purpose, you need to become a chef.

The Cook

There are a lot of advantages in being a cook and knowing how to follow a recipe. After all, that's how you learned to talk, walk, read, and write. That's how you learned math and science. You had to follow a recipe to get anywhere in life. Recipes are like rules. You need to know them in order to survive. Let's take a look at some important attributes of a cook:

- Good at taking orders

- Good at following directions in the recipe

- Can really get things done efficiently and are rewarded for repetition at a faster pace

- Not encouraged to experiment with an already proven recipe

- Do not decide what's on the menu

- Often find themselves "heating up" what someone else prepared

- Little creativity

- Get more repeatable, consistently positive results (initially)

- Absolutely necessary for a certain set of employees and patrons

- Tend to have more of an employee mindset, but not wasteful

- The food is almost always good

Satisfaction comes from serving others with good food and lots of it!

In business, a cook is a fantastic employee who isn't expected to think outside their box or make creative improvements to the team. The challenge comes when a cook is expected to miraculously become a chef overnight.

In my work, we often do this same thing with newer people. In fact, we even refer to it as "following the recipe." *You aren't successful yet? Follow the recipe better. Still not working? Make a double batch!*

Then, once you reach a certain level of success, you are congratulated for all of your hard work at following the recipe to become successful. While you are still smiling at the accolades, you are patted (proverbially) on the back and told, "What got you this far won't get you to where you are going. Good luck with that!" No joke. That's exactly how it feels. Not very heartwarming. Not very helpful, either.

You are asked to magically become a chef, with no guidance on how to do it. Until now.

The Chef

To be clear, some people aren't asked or forced to be chefs at all. Instead, they truly want to be chefs and welcome the idea. The challenge is in becoming versed in how to make this happen. Let's start by looking at what makes a chef different from a cook:

- Create exciting, unique meals—true experiences for their patrons

- Challenge tastebuds in new ways

- Take much more time to make each dish new and unique

- Inefficient in their methods (initially)

- Don't mind failing, as it happens frequently

- Determine their own menu

- Often start with an existing recipe and change/alter/amend one ingredient at a time to test it

- Once a new recipe is formulated, chefs direct the various cooks in how to make it—often dividing the responsibilities

- Have more of an employer mindset with a take-charge attitude, but not always when it comes to efficiencies and expenses

- Satisfaction with the process of creation and the impact on others.

The key to becoming a chef is being willing to open your mind and embrace change. You don't throw out the old recipe—you merely tweak one or two ingredients at a time and see how it works. If you like it, you know what impact that one change will have on the overall flavor. If it doesn't work, you know not to try that same combination again. By making small, incremental changes in this way with various areas of your life—in pursuit of your purpose—you are able to create an amazing and impactful life and purpose.

Bravery is about doing something even though you are afraid. Change is often scary. Becoming a chef can require both bravery and an Experimenter's Mindset. Be brave . . . and let's start experimenting!

16. The Experimenter's Mindset:

Finding Your Way

The importance of the Growth Mindset is not getting stuck in mediocrity. The Growth Mindset means that you are making constant, incremental improvements to grow. An Experimenter's Mindset is just as important. An experimenter is constantly trying new ways and combinations to see what works and what doesn't work at all. While there are reasons why an experiment doesn't work, there are no excuses.

Many times you will find far greater gain and benefit from getting past your desire to force a single solution.

In a recent reading of Grant Cardone's book, The *10X Rule*, he says that

"our success depends on our ability to increase our efforts—not our excuses."

That's true. Stop making excuses and start putting in the effort. If you have big dreams, you'll have to put in the work needed to reach them. There is no fairy godmother or genie, no magic lanterns or wands, that will suddenly make all your wishes come true. This is life, not a fairytale with a Brothers Grimm twist.

The Grand Canyon: How to Get There from Here

Let's look at one analogy in particular that will help put it in perspective—a visit to the Grand Canyon. Imagine that you are standing at the top of a cliff, near the edge. You look across the chasm and see all the things you wish for on the other side— your health, finances, relationships, career aspirations, and so much more, all over there waving and beckoning you to come. There is no bridge, no magic carpet to take you to the other side.

If you take a giant step to reach the other side right now, will you make it? No. You'll fall to your death on the rocks far below. Then how do you get to the other side where you so desperately want to be? You know that getting there will put you soundly on the path to your purpose. You know you need to fulfill your purpose. It's exasperating. You fall to your knees in frustration, head bowed, defeated.

You are different than most people. Their eyes would be closed, welling with tears, hopeless. Your eyes are wide open, and it is right now that you look around. Scattered all around you— previously unnoticed because of the beauty and call of those things you want across the chasm—are hammers, nails, boards, and other needed tools to build a bridge. It's then that you realize that building the bridge to carry you to the other side is your responsibility, your privilege, and a foundational part of your purpose.

Those tools and supplies represent the skills and abilities you need to develop to reach what's on the other side. You have to build this bridge one board and one hammer-strike at a time. It's up to you. As you get started, you realize that each board you place is important. You are aware now that you no longer just *wish* for what's on the other side. You *know* that you will have it.

The placement of each board is critical. You put a board six inches lower than your previous (i.e. you fall behind in developing that skill). You tell yourself that you will make it up tomorrow when you place the next board, then fail to do it. What happens if this continues? You'll end up building a staircase going down with little chance that you'll be able to build it back up in time to reach the top of the other side.

This represents the "efforts instead of excuses" that Cardone mentions in *The 10X Rule*. Keep your boards on the right trajectory to reach the top of the other side. Building consistently is easier than trying to make up for past excuses and laziness. This is why so many people give up. They see their trajectory is off and quit.

If this happens, as it often does, what do you do? Easy! See it early and you can build a small staircase to get you back to the proper height. Wait too long and it will indeed be too steep to climb.

Develop your skill-set in the critical areas and you will find that the journey to accomplishing your goals, and ultimately your purpose, will be just as fulfilling as when you finally achieve them. You will stop long enough once you reach the other side to celebrate the journey that got you there, pick up your accomplishments, and move on to even higher ground.

The joy is often not in the achieving of the goals but the realization of what an amazing journey it was that got you there. The journey makes you who you are. Never begrudge your past—you can't change it anyway—or the path you've taken so far. Use it to enhance your path and your purpose.

My friend, Katie, told me that she doesn't want to "unpack and move in" to where she is (the other side of her own Grand Canyon) because she needs to keep stepping it up. I love that! Don't unpack and move in to simply admire where you are. Reaching one goal is not your new residence or even an extended-stay hotel. It's a one-night stay before you gather up the new skills you have and move onward and upward like Katie.

The difference between a groove and a rut is simple. Are you going UP or DOWN?

Where are you right now? Are you still in "wishful thinking" mode? People who stay there grow bitter comparing themselves to others who have what they want. They rarely look closely enough to see that others have been busy building their own bridges. Are you on your knees crying because you don't have that magic carpet to carry you across and no one will build you a bridge? Get over it and develop the skills to get there. Wipe your eyes and look around. Begin filling your toolbox.

Others are working, one board at a time, to bridge the chasm to reach their goals. You can, too. Have you picked up a hammer with no idea where to start? Look around to see how others are working on and developing their skill-sets to build their bridges. Don't scoff at them and their skill development. Learn from them and others. Be a sponge and read on.

17. Defeating Villains and Super-Villains

I was going to title this chapter "The Monsters We Put Under Our Beds That Won't Go Away . . . Because We Feed Them!" Both chapter titles are appropriate. We do create many of our own monsters, or Super-villains, and we feed them—even nurture them at times.

What types of monsters and villains do we create? There are many. We get into cycles that drive us nearly mad. Many of us give in or give up, throwing up our hands in self-proclaimed defeat. These villains and Super-villains come in many forms, both internal and external. It's easier to tackle a villain first, so let's begin there.

Villains

1. Debt and Lifestyle Villains

Ben, a young man with hopes and dreams of finding his perfect career in a field that truly feeds his soul, bounds off to college in search of answers and opportunities. He starts his journey in the financial-aid office, where he takes out student loans to fund this new endeavor. Not knowing what he will need for sure, he takes out the maximum they offer him.

He goes to the enrollment office to register for classes. They tell him he needs to start with a few general education courses and that 12 hours is a full load for the semester, so he should focus on classes, not find a job. He enrolls and heads back to his new dorm room, where he's excited to meet new friends.

Fast-forward to five years later. Ben is still in college, has changed majors a few times, but he's finally landed on a degree he feels he can earn and is interesting to him—perhaps psychology, history, or art. When he took one of those early gen-ed courses, his professor told him he could be very good at it—and he was.

In the meantime, Ben found a group of friends who liked to go out together in the evenings and on weekends. He enjoyed their company so much that he had decided that one of his previous majors, perhaps finance, engineering, or architecture, was too hard and time-consuming to allow him enough time with friends. He dropped that major when he found out what work and dedication it required.

After being in college for nearly six years, amassing over $30,000 in student-loan debt (the approximate average debt as of 2015 data), Ben graduates with his undergrad degree. In his final semester, he spends much time and energy seeking appropriate employment in his field of study. He keeps hearing repeatedly that they are looking for students with graduate degrees and work experience.

Failing to find employment, and the prospect of debt repayment looming, Ben decides to pursue a graduate degree. Two years later with another $20,000 in student-loan debt, he graduates and finds a job in his field. It doesn't pay too well yet, but there's always the next job. This can be his stepping stone. As his student loans come out of deferment and payments are scheduled to begin, he realizes that this $50,000 debt load plus the need for a new car and other items to get him started are so costly that he can't afford housing.

Like 29% of the population between the ages of 24 and 34, Ben moves back in with his parents so that he can get a head start on paying his debts and building his future career. Ben has become part of the "boomerang" generation.

According to an article published in March 2012 by Kim Parker at the Pew Research Center, "Among the three-in-ten young adults ages 25 to 34 (29%) who've been in that situation during the rough economy of recent years, large majorities say they're satisfied with their living arrangements (78%) and upbeat about their future finances (77%)." Really? They live with their parents again. How do you think their parents feel?

Will Ben's debts be gone soon? Unlikely. Is Ben likely to see a large raise in pay soon?

Probably not. Will Ben's spending habits and desire to hang out with friends change? Doubtful. In fact, for many, the college years are just the beginning of the cycle of choices that lead them down a long, stressful path away from financial independence.

Those hopes and dreams and positivity people have in their youth often languish (and sometimes die) under the weight of massive debt in the basements of parents' houses or in the lavish homes they sometimes purchase that ultimately seal their fates as lifelong debtors. They purposefully, knowingly sell themselves into slavery. It's a slavery to debt, to a paycheck, to an employer, and often to negativity and cynicism.

2. The Viable-Excuse Villain

Each and every one of us is born with the ability to make our own choice. It's called free will. You must *own* those choices. Beware: there are at least as many excuses and rationalizations out there as there are choices. It's a trap.

As Dr. Jason Selk and Tom Bartow outlined in *Organize Tomorrow Today*, one of the biggest traps into which people fall is that of finding a viable excuse. It sounds good, pacifies a need to feel better, and prevents the negative emotions and mental repercussions of poor choices.

Have you ever failed to hit a goal at work and told yourself and others that it was too hectic to get it all done and still find time to meet that large goal? Ever failed to achieve something amazing in your life and justified your failure by saying and thinking that most other people aren't capable of doing it either? Ever have a friend who is "lucky" and always seems to have the right connections when you don't? Did the kids take too much energy out of you this morning? Fail a test because you're not a good test taker? All excuses.

Some of these excuses are what Hal Elrod in *The Miracle Morning* refers to as self-limiting beliefs. Others fit Brian Johnson's (brianjohnson.me) definition of Kryptonite, those things that seem to weaken us repeatedly. Regardless of how you define them, they are all excuses for not following through on your obligations. They keep you in a mediocre life. They keep you from becoming *Super*.

3. Needy Villains with Narcotic, Neurotic Wants

Repeated poor choices are very similar in some ways to a narcotic. Doubtful? Let me share an example of what happens every day.

A woman, exhausted with her daily grind, goes to the mall. She walks from store to store, spending hefty amounts of money for things she doesn't need. She does this routinely. She jokes with friends and family about being a shopaholic. She laughs. Her friends laugh and come with her on her shopping excursions. They laugh and they spend together.

What's really happening behind the scenes? She chooses many of the work-and home-stressors that she endures. She chooses not to take time for her own personal growth and development. She feels overwhelmed because she is expected to take care of her family, make sure their home is in perfect order, and get the kids to all the "right" activities on time. She feels like a hamster on a wheel, her legs running furiously yet getting nowhere. She is overwhelmed. She feels that she spends all of her time taking care of others and no one takes care of her . . . until she hits the mall.

At the mall, the store clerks have dollar signs in their eyes as she rolls into their store. Even if they didn't know her already, she's an easy mark—only just arrived and already carrying a large assortment of shopping bags. But she doesn't see these dollar signs—and if she does, so what? Finally, someone is there to wait on her, to be at her disposal. And it's about time!

This is a constant routine. Many of the new clothes in the closet go unworn, labels tucked inside so no one will notice but her. She gets a quick, fleeting sense of satisfaction from the service she received and the new items she has purchased.

Then that feeling of elation is gone and she feels unfulfilled again. She knows she has to face the bill when it arrives. This rampant spending creates friction in the marriage, and arguments ensue. In some cases, she'd like an argument. At least she wouldn't feel numb for a while. After all, that's the problem to begin with—she feels numb.

What could she have chosen instead? Perhaps she could've sat down and taken a look at what is really most important to her, most likely her family, marriage, possibly her career. She could have talked with her husband, who loves her deeply, and discussed how she feels and what's most important to them.

They could choose to work out a plan for self-improvement and empowerment for her, work through what each family member can do to remove some of her perceived load and contribute to the team. Together, they could cast a family vision. Maybe it's as simple as pursuing a few self-care routines, like an hour a day to herself to take a fitness or education class. Or simply to read or take a nap.

And there you have it. She has defeated her needy villain, her own chosen narcotic, and has taken steps toward fulfilling her super-powered purpose.

4. The Hypocrisy Villain

Many people aren't aware of the term "self-care," and certainly aren't aware of its importance. In order to fulfill your purpose, it often starts with working to fulfill that purpose within yourself. The flight attendant says that "in the event of an emergency, be sure to affix your own mask before helping others with theirs." How can you expect to take care of others properly if you aren't taking care of yourself?

It's baffling to meet parents who want their children to be more physically fit or have more self-discipline, respect, or confidence . . . when the parents refuse to work on these things in their own lives. All too often, the child is merely mirroring what they see in their parents. The disrespectful child with the belligerent parent. The chubby kid with obese parents.

The kids notice the hypocrisy. In a recent video online, I saw a mother screaming "encouragement" to her son to do more and better sit-ups and not to stop until he could do no more. I knew this mother years ago. She was overweight and did not exercise. As long as I'd known her, she'd done nothing at all to exercise or improve her physical condition (and there were no medical reasons why she could not).

Remember to use your PURPOSE as a litmus test for your actions, activities, and choices in other areas as well. It should guide you. Do you want your children to grow up to be healthy, responsible people? Then lead them by being a living example. Do you want to encourage and inspire people to reach for their full potential? Then you must reach for yours and accept no excuses along the way.

If we know these are bad for us, why do we feed them? If you look carefully at the story above or think of yourself or others you may know, you will notice there are several points where choices were made that continued (and even worsened) the situation. Many people give up on their dreams and goals and give in to the despair of their situation. When others are successful, it makes them feel worse. They may even try to tear away at other people's success.

The saving grace is that you can always change the choices you make. You can make new choices and form new habits. You got yourself into this problem with your choices, and you can *choose* to get out! To affect these changes, you need a change of mindset.

The topic of mindset brings us to the next set of villains: SUPER-villains. These are "Super"-charged because they are much more personal and insidious. They often become part of the fabric of how you view yourself.

Super-Villains

You want to be happy. You want to make a powerful difference in the world. You want to succeed at helping others. You want to live your purpose. You can be great, and you know it.

But you keep hitting roadblocks. Your brain is foggy. You tried the exercises earlier and are still struggling with finding or believing your purpose. What is happening to you? Why should something so simple be so hard? Perhaps the question answers itself. It's hard *because* it's so simple!

I've helped numerous people through the process through my coaching. Let me help you as well. I've included the following as a partial list of what can hold you back from making the choices that allow you to reach your potential. This is just a beginning and not meant to be exhaustive. The ideas below should jumpstart your thought processes so that you can better identify what affects you personally. Once you've read the list, add to it and make it your own.

These are mental blocks to success. Most people have them. Some even have layers upon layers of mental blocks. When you find your path through them, you will be far stronger. You will be well on your way to being Super.

1. Lack of Focus & Interruptions

Soundbites, commercials, smartphones, Facebook, Twitter, email—among many other items—have shortened attention spans and provided more distractions than ever before. And these are not the only distractions. It could be a coworker who can't seem to get motivated to work and insists on talking to you instead. Often what we allow to be uploaded into our brains is negative—whether it be newscasts, Facebook, Twitter, or conversations with negative people.

Not all of the distractions are external. With soundbite-length attention spans, people often distract themselves through random thoughts. The inability to get deeply involved in a project—even those meant for career advancement or personal development—is epidemic. People distract themselves.

You *choose* to turn off or leave the cell phone elsewhere. You focus on your most important work at a time of day when you are less likely to have interruptions. You time-block your days' activities to ensure that you have consistency. You tell your coworker that you need to focus. Instead, people often *choose* to let themselves become distracted with rationalizations and excuses, because it's usually easier for them not to get the work done—the path of least resistance will lead you nowhere.

Whether the interruptions are internal or external, you still have control over them. It may require changing the way you operate.

What got you to where you are
is unlikely to get you where you want to be.

Ditch the excuses. Choose to change and you will see tremendous progress in your life.

2. Wasteful Conversations

How often do you have conversations with coworkers or clients that really create no value? Likely, too often. If your conversations are purposeful, you will be able to accomplish far more. Your work will be smoother and coworkers and clients will understand that, when you engage them in conversation, it will *not* be a waste of their time.

It will create value in your relationships. They will start engaging you in a similar, value-creating way. Do this with your friends as well and you will improve your friendships.

The key is to be present as well as purposeful. Reduce the small talk and enhance the big talk. "Big talk" means that you are engaging at a deeper level, focusing on their needs, interests, and questions—instead of what you have to say. Dale Carnegie outlined it years ago in his book, *How To Win Friends and Influence People*. It's pure brilliance!

Why take the time to have deep, meaningful conversations at all? Doesn't that keep you from the rest of your to-do-to-be-successful list? Not at all! You can learn so much from others by knowing them more deeply. It will enrich their lives and make it possible for you to enrich your own as well. Avoid the wasteful, shallow conversations and your eyes will open to new possibilities.

If you find yourself attempting this and the other person is persistently negative, consider if you feel your time and energy are worth trying to change their attitude. If not, you may need to end the conversation and possibly end the relationship. More on this in a later chapter.

3. Fear of Success and Other Mental Gremlins

Many people actually fear success. Sounds crazy, doesn't it? Well, it does until you start to see yourself in it. Then it's crystal clear.

Successful people own (and sometimes choose) our neuroses— let's not fool ourselves, we all have them! Successful people own our neuroses, pack them in our luggage (it's luggage, not baggage, because we chose it), and proudly carry it through life. Unsuccessful people have baggage that sits on their shoulders, weighing them down.

SUCCESSFUL people put their luggage down and stand on top of it to reach greater heights!

I share this so you know that it's okay to have issues, quirks, and idiosyncrasies. It's normal and does not need to hinder your success. The ultimate question is: Do you own your neuroses, or do they own you? Successful people are more aware of themselves and do not live in denial. They are constantly looking to make incremental improvement in themselves.

Unsuccessful people either live in denial of their neuroses or allow themselves to be held back by them. You've probably met someone who is unable to get past what happened to them as a child, or brag about how they are a realist, or verbally destroy others to make themselves feel better.

Once you get past your most basic issues, you get into deeper waters. Several mental blocks associated with the fear of success run deep. They live in your blind spots. Have you felt that you desperately want to be successful but can't seem to get over that hump or that hurdle?

Chances are that you don't even fully know what the hurdle between you and your success is. In my coaching experiences, I've discovered several. It's only after you recognize your mental blocks, your blind spots, that you can fix them. Here are a few.

A. Blue Collar vs. White Collar

This was my own hurdle. I discovered it while doing an exercise with my business coach. It was designed to help me identify my motives and motivations. I realized that, while I grew up in a blue-collar world (my parents owned a plumbing, heating, and air-conditioning business), I was working in a very white-collar world.

As a financial advisor, I wasn't expected to do any hard manual labor, or even get a little dirty on the job. This made me feel very unworthy of my income. I felt that I needed to work long, hard hours like my parents had done.

This wasn't logical and, on some level, I knew it. That doesn't mean it was an easy hurdle for me to jump. I set out to unpack this crazy thing that was getting between me and my desired level of success. I discovered that the heart of the issue was *guilt*.

I felt guilty that I was not physically exhausted at the end of the day. Sure, I was mentally and emotionally far more tired than I remember being when I did manual labor, but where was the physical exertion? This tied into my guilt that my income exceeded what I knew many others earned. Why was I any better?

I'm *not* any better than they are. I simply have a different skill-set. It doesn't make me better than them or vice versa. It makes us different—that's all! Once I realized this, I started approaching my friends who do more manual labor from a different perspective. I was able to go out of my mind and into theirs!

I was able to value them for their skill-set and move well past that to learn and discover how amazing many of them were. In a few cases, we even inspired each other to work to achieve more! I annihilated my guilt.

B. Fear of Greed

Another common issue that I find when working with the people who I coach and mentor is that they don't want to be greedy. It's actually quite prevalent, though I failed to understand why at first. Let me give you an example.

While coaching Bill, I witnessed him build the systems and processes to be successful and hit all of the marks that he needed for that success. Then he seemed to self-sabotage and fail to hit his goals at the last minute.

I knew there was more to it than just having "bad luck." After all, you usually create your own luck. When Bill and I discussed what was happening and why, the answers started to come rapidly. Bill, as a strong Christian, felt that if he was very financially successful that he was being greedy.

That gave me a wonderful opportunity to share with him the stories of some of the firm's top producers. One gentleman, for example, who is one of the larger producers in the firm, lives a very modest lifestyle, spends plenty of time with his wife and kids, and they donate well over half of his annual earnings to charitable causes.

Another financial advisor who is extremely successful, along with her husband, personally funds a string of orphanages in Central and South America.

Both of these examples are people who live to use their skills and abilities to earn so that they can serve others. They also happen to be two of the biggest encouragers of others within our firm.

Bill decided that fear of greed was his issue and that he felt he hadn't given back as much as he should. He felt guilty about his current level of success. He spoke with his wife and worked out a plan to change that. Now he strives for greater levels of financial success so that his family can help to make more of an impact on the world—not because they want more stuff. He defeated his guilt.

C. The Win–Lose Mentality

Have you ever met someone who is so competitive that they make everything into a competition? Even though they may tone it down at times, they haven't changed their thinking.

They've just stopped being so vocal about it. Competitiveness has its time and place and can be a vital part of the world today. So why not have a win– lose mentality?

When interacting with someone who has a win–lose mentality, you quickly realize that if they win, you lose. It doesn't feel good to know that their objective is to defeat you repeatedly. It gets old fast and you stop working or associating with them. Their friends become distant, until they lose them entirely. When you have a win–lose mentality, you realize that openness makes you vulnerable. Vulnerability is a weakness. Weakness means you lose. After all, aren't the win–lose people always looking to gain the advantage? Find their opponent's weakness and exploit it?

What does this do to you, if you are the one with the win–lose mentality? Well, life is lonely. You learn to tone it down because, at some level, you realize that you shouldn't be that way. This realization often leads to feelings of guilt when you win (i.e. succeed). If you win, that means that the other person loses.

As strange as it seems, this has been the most common mental block for the people I coach. They tend to be goal-and result-oriented people who are always striving to do more at some point in their lives. It's particularly common among salespeople.

Derek was a former athlete who moved into a high-power, highly political career after college, and a man who lit up whatever world he touched. He was caring, empathetic, and driven. Six years into his post-college job, seeing the petty politics and gamesmanship practiced there made him bitter. That's when he decided to leave to start his own business. He was a slower starter than expected, but showed dogged determination not to quit.

I knew him while he was a student at the university where I taught. When he asked me to coach him, many years after those college days, I was both honored and surprised.

He wasn't the same man anymore. He wasn't driven. He settled for what came his way. He didn't strive to do and, most importantly, to *be* more. He had grown numb after the disenchantment of working in such a political position.

I brought this to his attention and reminded him of who he *used* to be. His years in his early career taught him that if one person wins, the other loses. He was disenchanted, numb, and drifting.

After just a few reminders of the amazing impact he'd had on the lives of his clients and their families, he started to see that it was really a win–*win* situation to work with him. The numbness started to fall away as we began to find ways that he could intentionally change his viewpoint in everyday activities.

Now that he has a win–win mentality, all of his relationships are stronger—friends, family, clients, and coworkers. He continues to work to regain that edge. It took more than six years to build that win–lose mentality in the first place, and it will take at least as long to get rid of it.

Try rearranging the players. If, for example, you view the other party (clients, customers, friends, etc.) as being on your team, you are more likely to be able to overcome many of the issues associated with a win–lose mentality.

I do this on a daily basis as I position myself as a partner/teammate with my clients. The rest of the investing world is the other team, and we work together to win at this game. As simple as it sounds once you hear it, the concept can change the dynamic of what you do daily.

In the end, the *guilt* of making others lose weighs you down. Derek slayed his guilt-villain.

What guilt-villains do you have? How can you defeat them? There are many and they can be found hiding in the shadows. Stay alert.

What on Earth is Wrong with You?

Do you remember my distinction between successful and unsuccessful people? Whether it's guilt, fear of success, a diagnosed (or even undiagnosed) psychological disorder, OCD tendencies, ADD, ADHD, or a host of other issues, remember that you are both the sum of your parts and have the potential to be far more than just the sum of those parts.

Your neuroses define who you are, if you allow them to. If you can understand and come to embrace them in a positive way, finding the opportunity in each, you will be able to reach far greater heights.

I'm a little OCD (as my husband likes to remind me) and a little ADD. That is a strange combination that ultimately means: "Oh look, a squirrel! Here, let me straighten those nuts!" Neither of these are clinical diagnoses—not to trivialize actual clinical patients living with OCD or ADD. But mine don't need to be, because they don't hold me back. In fact, I use them to my advantage in daily life. How? Well, I am organized and have a brain that lives in overdrive.

I develop systems to maintain high levels of routine and organization to my day, then I hand it off (at the office, at least) to someone else to manage the system. I find running my systems to be tedious. My team members, on the other hand, *love* systems implementation.

I also keep a notepad and pen with me wherever I go, even when I go for a walk. I never know when a random, inspirational idea will hit. I am known for walking into work "on fire" with some new idea that just hit me.

These ideas have changed my life for the better many times. My only regret is that I didn't know how to handle my neuroses at a much earlier age. Just imagine all of the ideas that my squirrel-mind forgot over the years because I was distracted by another "nut." Oh, well. I don't beat myself up over it. That doesn't serve any purpose, so I move on to the next nut.

Those of us who *own* our neuroses are often asked, "What on earth is wrong with you?" In fact, we don't even need people to say it anymore. We can read it in their faces as they look at us.

Let me be very clear in how to answer them. "Nothing is wrong! Everything is right . . . so very, very right. In fact, it's as if I have a Super Power. That power propels me forward because I allow it. Try to keep up if you can!"

Own those things that make you different from everyone else. You are unique. Choose to own what makes you different or it will own you. Remember, it is a Super Power. Be sure to use your Super Powers for good and never for evil. Be the Superhero, not the Super-villain.

18. Battling the Everyday and the Extreme

Most people want to prosper—especially in living their purpose—in the face of adversity. You want to persevere through it and come out stronger on the other side. You hear stories of people who have overcome adversity and want that for yourself. Maybe you've already done it and aren't sure how. Let's work to make it a part of your DNA.

Adversity

Adversity, as defined by the Merriam-Webster Dictionary, is "a difficult situation or condition." It is also defined as "misfortune." Fortune, in this context, means "luck." You may be familiar with the expression that the harder you work, the luckier you get. There's a lot of truth to that. Some people are able to create their own good luck through hard work, dedication, and seeking opportunities. By contrast, *misfortune* means bad luck. "Luck," for the most part, follows the pattern of our choices.

Bad things do happen to good people, regardless of choice. Merriam-Webster's adversity, "a difficult situation or condition," applies more than luck or fortune in some cases. Adversity doesn't always come to you because of bad choices that you make, and even when it is the result of poor choices, you still have the ability to use it to prosper.

You do, however, have the choice of how you *respond* to what happens to you. When you react instead of respond, you are operating out of a place of more raw emotion. That usually doesn't end well. Someone says something that triggers an immediate, off-the-cuff reaction in return. It's almost a knee-jerk reaction, an instinctual defense. You later wish you hadn't said it or you try to justify it. This is typical when you operate by reacting instead of responding.

What other choice do you have? You can find opportunity in most situations, learn powerful lessons from the incident, or even use it to leverage your strengths. You do this by not saying the first thing that comes to mind. *Breathe* for a moment, *listen* to what was said, and *understand* that others often operate from an emotional state without realizing it. Remove the thought that it's personal and choose to respond from a place of calm. Remember to go out of your mind and into theirs, and this will help you to choose a response.

You can change your relationships and change yourself by choosing to respond. It's the beginning of reframing your view of adversity. Try it. It's a fascinating exercise.

Prosperity

Some believe prosperity means money, belongings, living the proverbial "high life." A more meaningful definition of prosperity is having more than you need (though possibly not everything you want), enjoying fulfilling relationships, and having less anxiety and stress over what you cannot control. It also means being both satisfied with what you have and who you are and simultaneously continuing to strive for incremental improvements.

How do you do this?

Simple. Stop focusing on the results of your performance (i.e. income, net worth, possessions). If you focus on your systems and processes instead, you get more consistent results. Processes free you from the extremes of the rollercoaster of life.

Processes/Systems → Consistency → Prosperity

Short-term benefits include having clearer direction on where you are going and what you need to do today to get there. Long-term results will include more consistent performance and growth. Here are a few applications.

1. **Pour into our kids:** If you are consistent in interactions and expectations of your kids, you get more consistent results. Children are always pushing the limits with parents and other adults.

For example, if you greet your children after school or work with a frown on your face while looking at your phone, how should you expect them to greet you in return? Build a habit of ignoring your kids and they will ignore you. Treat them equitably and they will treat others in that way as well. Get frustrated and they will go to frustration immediately.

They are fantastic mirrors. By paying more attention to them, you will see the growth in yourself (or the lack of it) as well.

> ✗ *Consistent interactions lead to consistently prosperous relationships.*

2. **Put your best foot forward at work:** When you focus and pay careful attention to what or whom you have in front of you, you will get much more consistent results. Salespeople are particularly prone to inconsistency in results.

   Here's the cycle. She works hard, consistently doing the hard work she needs to do to get results . . . for a month or two. The results are fantastic and have worked so well that she takes them for granted and stops putting in the same level of work. She spends her time justifying that she deserves the time off or the lighter load, spending the money she worked so hard to earn and losing the momentum she built. Her inconsistent processes lead to inconsistent results.

Consistently implemented processes lead to consistent performance.

3. **Pursue passion:** You've always had the goal of writing a book, and you will start it when you have just the right inspiration. I once heard somewhere that 80% of Americans want to write a book. Few actually follow through on that desire. I have also heard this phrase: "Amateurs write when they feel inspired. Professionals write daily."

   The daily habit of writing, or doing anything worthwhile, is merely a process. When you get into the consistent process, it becomes much easier to get into flow with your writing. To borrow a phrase in theater, let's call it "getting into character."

   Do you want to write a book or take on some other large challenge? Set a process goal to complete a certain number of activities every day, including weekends and vacations, get into character, and you'll have achieved your goal far sooner than if you had waited for inspiration. That's prosperity.

   It doesn't have to be writing a book. There are many passion projects out there. Find where your passion resides and commit to pursuing it.

Processes, passion, and prosperity walk hand-in-hand (in-hand).

4. **Plan for the long term:** Retirement is another goal many people set and fail to systematize. Few people want to have to work in their current job for the rest of their lives. What does it take to be able to retire? It requires an alternate income stream. People need to save and invest toward their retirement years. In the 2010 US Census, people between the ages of 55 and 65 were surveyed. Of this group of people within 10 years of traditional retirement, 77% of them had less than $25,000 saved or invested in anything outside their homes.

   Why would the number be so low? Reasons and excuses abound, and many of those would seem quite viable. The key is that too few of us have a system or process in place to make it possible to accumulate the amount of wealth needed to sustain us in retirement. Those folks will be slaves to Social Security and likely have to keep working well into traditional retirement years—because they must, not because they desire to continue working.

   Have a process to consistently invest toward a work-optional lifestyle, and have a system to review your progress periodically. You will enable yourself to have this flexibility. Many people put off the important practice of saving and investing (a long-term need) for the short-term gratification of a new car, boat, vacation, or frequent trips to the mall. They trade lasting security for things that won't last at all. I'm not suggesting living a pauper's life. There can be balance.

It takes planning and intentionality to choose prosperity.

Prosperity is about much more than money. It's about designing your life to have more of those two limited resources—time and energy. Good choices are an investment in yourself, your family, and your future. What is the secret of a prosperous life? What will make your life prosperous? Now ask yourself, aren't you worth it? Dig in your heels and answer these questions.

- What does prosperity look like for you?

- Is it strictly monetary—better income, less debt?

- Or is it more closely related to the depth of your relationships with family and friends?

- Maybe it's building consistency in your personal or professional life?

- Or growing and developing yourself into becoming an even better person on a daily basis?

- Or . . . perhaps it's a mix of some or all of these things.

Advice from Others

No one else can ever determine what prosperity looks like for you. You can only do that for yourself. Others may try to push their definitions onto you, but you aren't free if you use other people's standards to determine what's important to you. When you try to use goals and norms others set, or live by their standards instead of your own, you don't own it.

You will never feel fulfilled achieving those goals, because they aren't yours. Living by their standards keeps you as a cook and doesn't allow you to become a chef.

People generally mean well when offering this kind of advice. At first, you might want to take it. You can certainly use their framework and build from it until you are confident in constructing your own framework. If their advice contradicts what you are trying to accomplish, however, you can choose to disregard it.

Be Abnormal

Let's take a moment to get back to the concept of adversity and how to face it. Once you have a clear idea of how you define prosperity, you will no longer be the "go-along-to-get-along" person that you were. You are aware of the choices others make and the impact these choices have on you and others. It's at this point that you need to remember the importance of responding from a place of strength instead of reacting from a place of emotion. Take a deep breath and move forward.

Most people operate in a way that keeps them where they are, maintaining the status quo. Many people think they are happy drowning in a sea of mediocrity. As Michael Bernoff says, most people are more afraid of losing something they already have than excited about getting something they desire.

Make no mistake: normal is boring. It doesn't change. Be abnormal. Abnormal means shedding the parts of the status quo that no longer suit you.

After you do, the adversity that invariably comes should be viewed as the fire that will mold and cast this new prosperous "you" in a more brilliant light. Depending on the people in your life and your areas of development, you will face resistance.

You will have people laugh at you. You may have self-doubt. Circumstances may arise, like the illness or death of a loved one, loss of a job, an unexpected move to another state or country. Stay tuned in to the opportunities that each of these present, both now and in the future.

Advice from the Grand Canyon: Welcome Your Challenges

Remember that the Grand Canyon was created because the water changed the rock, not the other way around. The Grand

Canyon is a wonderful illustration of how to uncover great purpose in the midst of adverse situations. You are just as majestic. If the Grand Canyon could speak, this is what it might give us as advice:

1. "It took thousands of years for me to form. It will take time for the new you to take hold and surround yourself with the people, practices, activities, and interests that suit you. Give yourself the time."

2. "I am not a straight path. When my waters met extreme resistance in the stone, they moved a bit and still persevered. When you have a negative person or activity in your life, move around it. Your best path may be away from people who cause trouble in your life. It's okay to take a winding path. In fact, as you grow personally, it's expected and natural."

3. "My waters do not stop. They keep flowing, no matter what gets in the way. Have your daily routines, processes and systems in place and follow them consistently and purposefully. Choose to give yourself the best chance to prosper."

4. "Long after my waters, which broke through the rock were gone, their impact on the rock has remained. Imagine, long after you leave, the effect that your persistence will have on others. I, the Grand Canyon, am grand, not because of the waters that flow through me right now, but because of the impact of the waters that flowed through me ages ago. You are the water tearing away at the edges of the rock to expose their beauty

while letting your own beauty shine as well. It may take a while for your true impact to be seen. That's okay. That's your legacy."

It is because of the adversity the water faced that the Grand Canyon is so majestic. Embrace your adversities and count them as blessings as you find opportunities in them. Give yourself permission to enjoy the process of seeking and achieving prosperity. After all, it really is about the water's journey.

Making choices—the good ones—doesn't mean you don't have to work to be successful. You do have to work. It means that your efforts are far more fruitful and your vision that much closer to being accomplished when you combine good choices with hard work. It means that your choices are made with a purpose in mind. They are fulfilling and enriching your life. You live a life without the regrets so many face with poor choices. You feel alive, not numb, to the world. Instead of always looking for your next thing that will make you feel alive, you are already alive and kicking!

Use your purpose as the litmus test by which everything is weighed, measured, and tested. Using purpose as a litmus test takes it from being a purpose to a Super Purpose. This is how a Super Power is born.

Embrace Your Path

Overthinking is the doom—the Kryptonite—of self-professed perfectionists. Understand that no solution or plan is perfect and, thankfully, it never will be! You are an ever-changing creation and have the amazing ability to grow, morph, and evolve your plans over time. There is exhilaration in that. Embrace it.

The more you overthink, the less action you take because you construct a plan far too complicated to achieve. To avert this, follow these three simple steps.

1. Simplify (Ready)

Boil it down to one or two things (preferably one) that you need to complete in order to put you on a successful trajectory. It may be a skill, an attitude shift, or simply picking up the phone. Bring it down to the basics. For a detailed version of how this works, check out Gary W. Keller and Jay Papasan's book, *The ONE Thing*, where they address this thoroughly and with brilliance.

2. Focus (Aim)

Once you know what you need to do to align yourself with your target, focus your sights very closely and let no distractions get in your way while you take aim to make the first shot. You need to pay keen attention to where your shot lands. That's the real benefit of focus. You need to see the impact so that you can make any corrections necessary.

3. Engage (Fire)

PULL. THE. TRIGGER. Few people actually complete step three. Nothing happens until this point, so any other work you put in is irrelevant unless you actively engage. Remember the point of focusing? Pay close attention to where you hit—or don't hit—the target. Did you miss? Get over it. It's not a personal indictment or reflection on your character. Refuse to fail by learning instead. Go back to your fundamentals and take aim again. Do what you need to do to get closer on your second attempt. Then continue to zero in on the bullseye.

Let's say your business is a martial arts school (an example I can speak of with authority). You need 20 new students this month. That will line you up for your goal of reaching 300 students by the end of the year. You recently attended a home show and had several people give you their contact information.

You know you need those 20 students to sign up this month and you have well over a hundred families to contact. Instead of overthinking what you will say, write a quick script with a few talking points and pick up the phone.

Wait! Did you forget to return an email to a supplier? Forget it. Do it later. Oh, no! Toilet paper is out again in the bathroom and students will be arriving in three hours. Stop. It can wait until after you've made 20 calls.

Do you see the issue we have with focusing? You allow distractions with every little excuse that pops into your head. You know that making these 20 calls is what needs to be done.

Focus is the name of the game. No distractions. You pick up the phone and dial. Someone answers. You fumble over a few words, but they are fairly receptive to what you have to say. After hanging up, you realize that you need to practice more so that you don't fumble over your words.

Who can you practice with? Mom! You call your mom to practice. Three hours later, after discussing everything except your practice calls, you hang up, change out the toilet paper, and go teach class. You got *one* call done, barely.

Is practice bad? Not at all. You just chose the wrong way to practice. Even if you role-played with her, Mom is not an ideal prospect and will be too nice to you or just unrealistic. It's best to course-correct with actual prospective students. This is how you build your confidence to continue making the calls. You figure out that people won't actually bite you (impossible over the phone anyway), you will survive, and you are improving.

Simplify. Focus. Engage. (. . . and keep engaging for as long as necessary!)

People often get strange, unfounded ideas in their heads about worst-case scenarios.

Over a decade ago, while assisting with training new financial advisors, I realized that they were petrified at getting out and meeting new people. The training involved a week-long (Monday through Friday) class engaged in extensive role-play to get them comfortable approaching strangers at their doorstep and introducing themselves. As I sat there, it occurred to me that role-playing with each other was far too easy. They were being really nice to each other. Unrealistically nice.

After a brief discussion with the professional trainer (I was merely a volunteer), I wrote a schedule on the board at the front of the class. I told them that they each needed to sign up to do a role-play with me at my hotel room that evening. They didn't understand, since they were new, that this was far from the norm of what usually happened at the class.

As each arrived and knocked on my hotel-room door that night, I gave each of them a very different scenario. I gave them real scenarios and several that were even a little over the top (i.e. pretending to be a five-year-old answering the door—it happens). The result of forcing them into an uncomfortable position outside the cozy setting of the training facility was that they realized that they would survive and that their worst fears wouldn't likely be realized.

The more time they allow their fears to take over, the bigger those perceptions of what will happen become. By nipping this fear in the bud on the first day, the rest of the week was fantastic. They couldn't wait to get out and meet people. They began to see it as I see it—an adventure behind every door.

This forced engagement outside of their comfort zones was just what they needed. They needed it early, before fears could set in too deeply, and you do too.

What can you do right *now* to get you past a fear that may be stopping you? Tackle it head on and you'll find that it wasn't that bad after all. It never is. Own your fears through *action* and *engagement* and they will never own you. It's your choice.

19. Kryptonite Kills, Sunshine Heals

Once you work through what holds you back, it doesn't always mean that you are home free. You may have decided to become a Superhero, but you need to beware of the Kryptonite. It's everywhere.

There is still the need to shut out much of the negative in the world so that it doesn't drag us back down with it. I turned off the news well over ten years ago when I realized that all they do is recycle the same garbage into more garbage. Don't misunderstand—I like recycling . . . when they come up with something useful on the other side. Just rehashing the same negative, tired news can be downright disheartening. It's like a Goliath of negativity against our David-sized positivity, optimism, and courage. If we don't tackle it head on, it will take us down a very negative road. My choice was to turn it off. All of it.

It's not just the news that can hinder your energy. It is often the people in your life. Remember that you choose whom you let into your life and what energy trail they leave behind.

I know a person who just wants to be negative and argumentative all the time. Do you know someone like that? I don't have to be around her much, thankfully, and I choose not to let any of her negativity follow me after we talk. Her problems are her problems because she continues to choose to let them be her problems. It is interesting how many people let her problems become theirs. They stew and brood and stress over them. I choose not to live that way.

You choose the energy you allow to affect you, to make the most of what you can control, and to respond (not react) in a way that feeds and strengthens you.

That's where the Positive Energy Challenge begins. It begins by identifying both your crippling Kryptonite and your healing Sunshine. This is a simple exercise to understand. The challenge is in implementation. Take it one step at a time and be careful not to skip ahead. Here is how it works.

1. Identification: Energy Boosters (Sunshine)

Take a close look at your daily habits and interactions. Figure out the activities, people, and interests that give you peace, joy, growth, and passion. In other words, they give you energy and help you feel fulfilled. They are often related to your purpose. These are the people and experiences you want *more* of in your life. We will figure out how to replicate these, hopefully exponentially, over the long term.

Make as thorough a list as possible. Be very specific about details and about how they make you feel. For example, to say that you love spending time with your children is too vague. A more specific answer could be that you enjoy spending time with your children playing for 15 minutes each day after work and listening to what happened in their day. You know that to make this time meaningful you need to greet them after school with a snack (low blood sugar equals cranky kids).

2. Identification: Energy Leeches (Kryptonite)

Now take a close look at what deprives you of joy, peace, hope, and energy. A leech is a blood-sucking worm that attaches itself to you. You have had experience with them, at least figuratively. These people are always negative or needy. It could also be circumstances, activities, events, places, Facebook, email, or a combination of the above.

You may like certain aspects (and are fed by them), but not other aspects. For example, you have a friend who is always negative about other people but says kind things to you. Or the friend who has major life issues, but you tolerate the drama because it makes you feel better by comparison.

You will need to make a very thorough list (and will likely keep adding to it) of what leeches the energy from you.

3. Liberate Yourself from Leeches

Some people are very negative. If possible, cut ties with them. You've heard of people who go systematically through their social-networking pages and

delete/remove/unfriend people who are negative. Unless your life's purpose is to turn all of these negative people into optimists and you are "fed" by that purpose, sever your connection. Break up with them both physically and emotionally. Deal with any emotions you have by examining your newfound liberation and replacing a toxic relationship with an enriching one.

What do you do if it is a family member, or something you are obligated to do for work or family reasons? Perhaps a coworker you have no choice but to work with? Or your next-door neighbor? Realize that you will never be able to change everyone and it may not be your place to try. Ultimately, it's *their* choice whether to grow and develop themselves or not.

What you *can* choose is how you will *respond* to them. You don't have to let their negative energy through your Teflon coating. Stay in their presence for as short a time as possible, setting clear expectations and a positive mood and tone right away. Minimize exposure to this Kryptonite.

Food for the Hungry

Let's step back for a moment to discuss the difference between what you "feed" into your life and what "feeds" off of you. Have you ever been hungry and eaten completely based on how something tastes? You ate so much that it bordered on gluttony and gave you a stomachache. It tasted so good when you took that first bite that the bites just kept coming. Maybe you even moaned and hummed while you ate the tasty goodness.

You couldn't stop, jumping from one tasty food to another. Finally, after binge eating, you can consume nothing else. The torment of the overwhelmed digestive system hits you full force, maybe even painfully. What were you thinking?

It is much the same way when you are surrounded by energy leeches. At first, it feels good. You think you can make a difference in their lives. They need you. Let's be honest—it feels very good to be needed and to feel that you have your stuff more together than someone else. It can be almost intoxicating.

After a while, though, you realize that these people are not really looking to change. They just want someone to talk to, gripe and complain to, someone who will listen. They never had any real intention of changing and improving. They were just happy to find you, their next victim.

They systematically wear people down and have to keep moving to some other generous soul.

You have allowed them to bring you down their road of negativity and you are a wasted shell. That's the equivalent of a seriously messed up stomach.

Now that you have listed the leeches, rate each of these energy leeches with a number between one and ten, depending on how you feel. Pretend you are about to encounter them. How will you feel in the midst of the interaction? How is your energy level once the encounter is finished?

One is your low score, meaning that it's more of an annoyance. A ten would mean that you need ample amounts of counseling, alcohol, or a lengthy vacation after the interaction. Put these in descending order with most-challenging leeches at the top and those merely annoying ones at the bottom. Start at the top and begin eliminating them.

Use the workbook at www.chooseyoursuperpower.com to list and score them.

- What can you do to either eliminate or minimize the largest of your leeches?

- How can you neutralize the effects or minimize the frequency of contact?

Develop a strategy to permanently change your life by removing these energy drains altogether, when possible, and at least minimizing their effects on you.

4. Actively Engage Energy Boosters

Replace the energy leeches with energy *boosters*. If you don't, you fall back into your old habits. Energy leeches become your comfort zone. You need to develop a new comfort zone that will help you make progress in living your purpose. *Energy* leeches are also *time* leeches, sucking away at both your time and energy.

Time and energy are your most valuable and scarce resources. You need to inject more positive energy into the available time in your life. Choose for it to be something that feeds you, fulfills your purpose, and creates excitement.

What feeds you, gives you energy, boosts your mood, and makes you feel fantastic? This applies to both mind and body. Look at what happens when you feed your body good, nutritious food that is also tasty. You feel mentally sharp and crisp. You are mentally stable because your blood sugar is not flying then crashing. Most importantly, you are bounding with energy. Your organs receive the nutrients they need. Your body is using all of the nutrients it receives more efficiently. The neurons in your brain are buzzing with greater speed and connectivity, giving you enhanced clarity.

You feel vigorous and alive. That's the same feeling you get when you surround yourself with positive, upbeat people who are working, striving, and reaching hard for their goals as well. Find people who know their purpose and strive to reach it. They are both empowered and empowering. They make your heart and soul sing, and in harmony with theirs!

These are your energy boosters. And they are not just people. They can be activities—like reading, journaling, meditating, exercising, volunteering, and so forth—that give you energy and a positive boost throughout the day.

Take the list where you identified your energy boosters at the beginning of this chapter; number and sort them as you did before with the other list. A score of ten means that it creates the most energy and vitality for you. A score of one is for those things that feed you only a little.

Deploy that list vigorously! Take it one item at a time so you don't get overwhelmed. Focus on *replacing* each energy leech with an energy booster. Work systematically to enhance your energy by incorporating more energy boosters in your daily life.

An interesting thing will happen. You will start to discover a new set of energy boosters. At first, this may surprise you. You will continue over time to see more opportunities to expand and explore your Super Purpose. You are blessed with the time, energy, and clarity of vision to see them.

Back to the food analogy (probably because I'm hungry as I write this). If you decide not to eat unhealthy foods, that's great. But your body requires that you replace those unhealthy foods. With what? Healthier foods, of course! The same principle applies here as well. You must focus on replacing the negative with the positive.

The old adage that "nature abhors a vacuum" is right. Don't believe me? Try not eating anything for a while because you only have junk in the house. You'll end up eating it anyway, because you have to feed your body something. In this case, you have to fill your *time* with something else or you will go right back to the wrong people and activities. We need purpose, direction, and good energy to be willing to shed the bad habits and energies of our past.

You can fill your time and feed your energy by building and creating tools for your toolbox. I recently heard a great idea: Give yourself a "Personal" MBA (master's in business administration) by constructing a list of 99 business books to read. If the Personal MBA isn't your thing, create a 99-book-master's course to living out your purpose in a more meaningful way. The opportunities are endless.

Need more ENERGY BOOSTERS? There are more ideas from other Supers on The Super Guild Facebook page. Be sure to share your ideas too!

5. Side Effects

Making these changes will involve side effects. So in the interest of full disclosure, here are a few of them.

- One woman I know severed ties with a very close friend because she was always very negative and demoralizing. She had tried to turn this friend around, but to no avail. Sounds like a great choice to me! After parting ways, she felt guilty and spent time "Facebook-stalking" her negative former friend. She was overwhelmed with the guilt and had not taken steps to fill her time with more positive energy.

The BIG G (guilt) will continue to haunt you if you let it. Remember my personal motto, "The devil lives in your comfort zone, and he likes it when you live there with him . . . so get out!" The negative energies, your energy leeches, live in your comfort zone, and they want to get you back in there. This is the most epic of Super Power battles.

- The second side effect is that, when the Positive Energy Challenge is properly employed, there will be people in your life—even those who are energy boosters—who will wonder "what on earth is going on with you." When I told my husband that I was going to write this book, I don't think he believed me. At Christmas, he shared it with his family and our nephew laughed at me and scoffed at the idea.

I grinned at my nephew and thanked him for inspiring me. After he gave me a quizzical look while I was frantically writing in my notebook, I said (reading from what I'd just written), "Small minds scoff at big ideas. They find them intimidating and are often threatened by them." Conversation and energy-drain *over*.

In fact, during a brief visit to us recently, that same nephew stood over my shoulder reading what I was typing about energy leeches. I love my nephew. He's usually one of my energy boosters.

Do those side effects sound like too much for you to handle? If so, here are a few other side effects to being a Super and living *with* purpose *on* purpose:

- Increased sense of fulfillment

- More focused attention and time for your family and friends

- Fewer sleepless nights

- Closer relationships

- Increased work and personal productivity

- More time to pursue your passions

- Greater focus on and movement toward fulfilling your life purpose

- Improved health

- Lower stress levels

- Enhanced mental clarity

- Less procrastination

- Greater freedom from debt, guilt, depression, and overall negativity

- More desire to eat frogs (*What?* Read Brian Tracy's book, *Eat That Frog*, to understand!)

Now that you're paying attention again, let me add that:

- Life will be more fun

- You will also regain your spunk, sense of humor, and desire to have fun!

Write down your Top 3 Energy Boosters and Leeches. Put them in order of getting them into or out of your life. Develop a clear strategy for eliminating or enhancing them and put that plan into action. Then cross off each leech once you have it completed. (I recommend using a big, wide marker to completely cover those leeches. Let's make sure they don't haunt us again.)

On the energy boosters, once actively engaged, hit them with your favorite color of highlighter! We still want to be able to see what feeds us. Make it a new habit to revisit these lists on at least a monthly basis so that you can continue to make progress.

New leeches will occasionally rear their ugly heads. Eliminate them swiftly. In those months when there are no additions to the leeches, celebrate keeping them at bay! You will also find, as you grow personally, that other practices and people who come into your life truly feed your energy levels. You will become a magnet, attracting other energy boosters by becoming one yourself. Be sure to stay on top of these new energy boosters too.

This entire Positive Energy Challenge is a choice—your choice. You may choose not to implement it at all. As long as you are making an informed choice, that's fine. Remember that you can always choose to implement it later. It's an awakening of awareness that you do have a choice.

If you choose to implement the Positive Energy Challenge, I would love to hear the results. Please share them by contacting me online at www.chooseyoursuperpower.com or through the Facebook group The Super Guild.

20. Mastering Your Secret Identity

You've been there:

Life is good. You've had several things go your way lately. You feel on top of the world.

Or perhaps you're on the bottom of the world, feeling miserable because no matter what you do, life just doesn't seem to be going your way.

These ebbs and flows are completely normal, but who wants to settle for normal? For some, more time is spent at one end than the other. If you are honest with yourself, you've been at both extremes.

Why do some people seem to lead a charmed life, while others feel the stress of failure and adversity constantly? As you've already discovered, much of that is based on choice and perspective, reaction or response.

If you choose to view your life as a series of obstacles, your outlook will stay generally negative and you will attract more obstacles.

If you choose to view your life as a series of opportunities, your outlook will stay generally positive and you will attract more opportunities. It's the Law of Attraction.

The question then is how to stay focused on opportunities?

1. **Have a Contingency Mindset**, as previously discussed. Know that life won't always be optimal. Be vigilant about looking for opportunities, especially when events occur that are out of your control.

2. Know Your Positioning

In coaching, I frequently cover the issues of POSITIONING and CONDITIONING. They are key to much of what happens and few people are aware of them. Nearly everything you do, say, and believe is about positioning and conditioning.

- You position yourself, your team, your family, your friends. As a financial advisor, for example, I position our team with clients and other professional contacts. Our team consists of the three people in our office, each with different skills, talents, and roles. We are all professionals and excel in our particular areas. We are cross-trained and able to help other members of our team for the benefit of our clients.

  We work alongside our clients to help them achieve their goals and desires. Our words, actions, and behaviors all align in order to reinforce this positioning as part of the team.

In fact, we refer to ourselves as Team Synergy, because together with our clients we are able to accomplish far more than any of us could do independently, no matter how good we each are.

- As a martial arts instructor, I position myself with students as an authority figure who cares about their growth and development, both on and off the mat. They feel comfortable interacting with me, even making requests for what they would love to do in class, while respecting that I am in charge of what happens. This is part of my positioning.

- A stay-at-home parent who homeschools children may have varied positioning with them depending on what activity they are involved in or what time of day it is. If the morning is their normal classroom time, the children will treat the parent as the teacher. After the schoolwork is completed, Mom or Dad may get on the floor and play actively with the kids. This positioning can be very distinct.

Positioning can be either intentional or unintentional, but it is always present. How are you positioning yourself in the various areas of your life—with your spouse, children, clients, coworkers, friends, and other family members?

How are you positioning yourself internally? While it's great to position ourselves with others, it's even more important to have a clear understanding of who we are internally—this is internal positioning. If you need to be outwardly confident in what you do, you must be internally confident as well. If you want to project and position yourself as a positive, upbeat person, you must believe that you are a positive, upbeat person.

Positioning may vary depending on which role you currently have—parent, professional, friend, or spouse. But they should still maintain a congruency. The difference from one environment to another has more to do with what parts of your personality are shining most brightly. If you are in a professional work setting, it may not be appropriate to show the same playfulness you would with your children. If you are on a date with your spouse, you may be better off showing less of a professional demeanor than you do at the office.

Are you allowing others to position you? I've seen many times that people allow their past or even other individuals to determine their positioning. You may be a titan at work, but as soon as your mother walks into the room you become the frequently scolded, ten-year-old version of yourself again. You run your household like the Amazon Princess, Wonder Woman, but as soon as you walk into work you cower in the shadows and hope not to be noticed. You've transformed into a quiet mouse.

Positioning isn't just about *who* you are. It's also about *where* you are. As you walk through the next week, consider how you are positioning yourself. If you walk into a meeting with a low-confidence positioning, what are the results? If you have family play-time and are very serious about getting results (i.e. winning the game or wrestling match), how does that impact the quality of your time together?

3. Conditioning

Conditioning and positioning are linked. Though positioning usually has to do with how you position yourself in relationships with others and how you view yourself, conditioning is more about how you set parameters when interacting with others. You condition others in what they can expect from you, and you establish expectations of them as well. It works this way in any well-established relationship.

- In a work environment, you have certain expectations of your coworkers and they have certain expectations of you. You may take a few breaks to chat during the day, even with your boss. However, when the CEO walks through the door, that changes immediately.

- When you greet someone, how do you do it? Do you shake their hand, smile, frown, give them a hug, or just nod your head? If you typically greet them with a warm smile, they become conditioned to this and start to smile whenever they anticipate seeing you. Try it. This practice requires some consistency. If you usually frown at people or avoid eye contact, you'll notice it takes a while to change their conditioning.

Conditioning needs to be consistent with positioning. This often happens without us even considering it. If you are the titan at work and visit your mother, for example (instantly transforming into your ten-year-old self), that positioning probably has a lot to do with your conditioning over many years.

Is it impossible to break the conditioning? No. Does it require conscious, intentional thought? Yes. Perhaps a breakthrough, on your part at least? Absolutely.

4. Repositioning and Reconditioning

I have had many circumstances over the years to reposition and recondition. Several years ago I had an opportunity to do this with my dad. When in a professional appointment with me one day, I was outlining the strategies that I was implementing. He leaned forward toward me with a perplexed look on his face, as if he didn't recognize me.

The words that followed changed our professional interactions and removed his skepticism (he still thought of me as his little girl, not the 40-something I am). "You're really brilliant, very good at this. Vicky, did you know she was so smart?" Vicky is my mom. She smiled and said she did know. Thanks, Mom and Dad!

The moral of the story is that you can effectively reposition yourself and recondition your relationships if you do so with intentionality. It usually requires making a conscious choice.

You need to figure out how you want to reposition first. What does this look like? Let's look at another example.

- Are you all talk and no action, or can people count on what you say? If you have long been the person who sets a goal to "get in shape" and everyone you tell looks at you with that "Yeah . . . right" expression, you have some repositioning to do. You've obviously already positioned yourself as someone who rarely follows through on what you start. You have conditioned them to expect little from you. Start the repositioning within yourself.

  What's going on inside your brain to keep you from finishing what you start? Are you willing to overcome it? You are certainly capable if you choose, but that's not the real question. Are you *willing*?

  If so, find new accountability partners if you need them. These partners are people who have already done what you plan to do, not people who will help you make excuses. Then get very specific about what your goals and desires are. You might even choose to work with this new partner to come up with the objectives.

  Why someone who has already succeeded? Simple. They are less likely to let you backslide into your old ways. But if you surround yourself with people who aren't much further along in many ways than you are, it's more comfortable and they are overly forgiving (so that you will let them off the hook later).

- Once you see measurable success, then those old friends and accountability partners will start to ask what you're doing. It's at this point that the reconditioning begins. They see that you look and feel healthier and more energetic. They may even want to emulate your success.

  As exciting as the accolades and encouragements are, you can't let them be the reason you are pursuing this goal. Those compliments are fleeting. Once they see you in the new light for a while, they will expect that you are a changed person with the intent to follow through on what you said you would accomplish. The reconditioning has begun.

  If you get off track and backslide again, it will be even harder to convince them that you've really changed. It further cements that old view of you. It's what they expected to begin with. This could set that reconditioning back again. It's important to be doing the right things in the right way for the right reasons.

When you try to recondition other people's expectations of you before you internally reposition and recondition yourself, you will often fall back into your old ways because they offer the path of ease, of least resistance.

In the end, the choice of how you position yourself and condition others is yours. Choose wisely.

21. Mastering Your Toolbox

It's time to gear up, to equip yourself with what you need in order to ensure your purpose becomes a Super Purpose. Jim Rohn, famous father of self-development, once said that you will never be able to out-earn your level of personal development.

I am always trying to develop my skill-set so that I have as big a toolbox as possible for whatever my next adventure may be. I recently had the opportunity to be part of a group coaching session, and "congruency" was a foundational topic of discussion. *Congruency* is integrity, where your words, thoughts, and actions are all aligned. The lessons learned throughout this coaching experience were fantastic. Thank you, Michael Bernoff!

- Is it congruent if your goal is to lose 20 pounds and you eat junk food? No, those don't go together.

- Is it congruent if you are in the health and fitness business and stand outside your business smoking cigarettes? No, definitely not.

Once you know what it looks like *not* to be congruent, you start to see it everywhere, even in yourself. The most damaging type of incongruency is when it comes to developing your skill-set and deepening your toolbox. It is the little stuff you do that others may not see.

Without having your thoughts and actions in alignment, or congruent, you will struggle to live within your purpose. Living your purpose on a daily basis requires confidence in both your purpose and yourself. How can incongruency be so devastating? Here's a common example.

- Let's say your goal is to lose those 20 pounds. You stop to gas the car and go in to pay cash. You get a discount for cash, right? When you go in, you notice all the candy bars near the register. You grab one, throw it on the counter, and walk out of the store with it. It's one candy bar, no big deal. You are starving and it will keep you from overeating when you get home—do you hear the excuses yet? You practically inhale it on the way to the car and toss the wrapper in the trash. No one needs to know. Except you. You know. That little incongruency, wrought with the excuses you tell yourself, just made you think of yourself as a liar, a fraud. You may not say the word "liar" to yourself, but you know that's how you feel.

- It may not be a candy bar and weight loss. It may, instead, be justifying constant online shopping when you are trying to build up your cash cushion. Or perhaps it's not making the calls at work because you just don't feel like it today. Or perhaps it's putting off that project you know you should do. You know the one . . . it's been on your to-do list forever.

Pick your goal and you can probably find an incongruency in your actions and attitudes. When you feel an excuse coming on, incongruency is there. If you don't notice yourself making excuses, congratulations on either maintaining a brilliant tool in your toolbox . . . or for being really good at fooling yourself.

Congruency is a choice. Sharpen and hone the skill of congruency by consciously looking at your choices and those made by others. Put them to that litmus test to see if they are congruent.

How do you try to justify your incongruencies? What excuses do you make to yourself and others? Congruency is one of the most valuable tools in your toolbox. If your ultimate purpose involves impacting other people, this may be your most valuable tool. Others need to see you walk the walk as well as talk the talk. And you need to see it in yourself as well.

Filling Your Toolbox

What else do you need in your toolbox? Your purpose and the short and long-term goals you set determine what your toolbox must contain. The items in your toolbox will be ever-changing. In fact, the *quality* of those tools will continue to improve as well. Here are a few standard tools needed to pursue your Super Purpose.

1. **Confidence** in yourself and your purpose. This doesn't mean that you should never question yourself or your purpose. You need to do those things at the right time and in the right way. Every Superhero has those defining moments when, after questioning their purpose, they come out much stronger and more focused on the other side.

2. **Compassion, Empathy, and Forgiveness** for others, as well as yourself. No one is perfect and no one can control everything that happens. A Superhero is bigger than holding grudges and judging others for events out of their control.

3. **Vigilant Focus** on pursuing improvement of yourself and others. The work is never done, and that's a good thing. Who wants to reach a point where they say, "Okay, this is as good as I will ever get. No more improvements to see here, folks"? Why settle for good, or even great, when you can be *Super*? Have your radar up for those opportunities!

4. **Awareness** of challenges and opportunities both internal and external. Looking for opportunities— instead of looking at people and events as obstacles—is a hallmark of what makes some people extraordinary. Find a challenge and you've likely found an opportunity to grow in some way. Engage it!

5. **Well-Crafted Communication** with yourself and others. How we talk to ourselves is as important as how we talk to others, if not more. You must understand the

impact of words, both spoken and thought. They have tremendous power. When it comes to making themselves bigger, there are generally two types of people in this world: those who try to tear others down to make themselves feel bigger; and those who lift others up so that they can reach greater heights. Be aware of your words, actions, and intonations, and the impact they have on others as well as yourself.

6. **Integrity and Congruency** in your words and actions. Integrity is choosing right over wrong, always . . . even when no one else is looking. Congruency, as previously described, is having your purposes, goals, and objectives lined up with your words and actions. Integrity and Congruency walk hand-in-hand. If you lack one, you have violated the other. Special care in this area is crucial in assuring that your goals can be reached and you don't feel like a liar or a fraud.

7. **Clarity** in your purpose. Though your purpose may grow and develop over time, you must have clarity in your purpose and a clear understanding of how each activity, or mission, fits into your purpose. If it doesn't feed into and align with your purpose, it will either pull you off-track or be remarkably unfulfilling. Neither is good and both are a waste of your precious time and energy.

8. **Growth-Oriented Mindset** is a key to maintaining emphasis on the other seven tools outlined above. It is only by continuing to grow, develop, and improve yourself that you will gain greater clarity of purpose so that you can continue to hone these other skills.

This requires that you develop a plan and strategy for how to stay on the path of continuous improvement. Have you ever noticed a time when you felt like you were mentally, possibly physically, unstoppable? Did you take the time to figure out what happened to make you feel that way? You must discover it if you want to be able to replicate it.

For me, that happens when I am feeding healthy fuel into my mind through reading, writing, coaching, interacting with the right resources and people. This feeds my energy and helps me grow tremendously as a person. It's when I stop doing these things that I become like a dull blade, having trouble cutting through the fog to see my purpose with clarity. It's then that my purpose starts to slide away from me and I begin to focus more on myself than on others. Therefore, the Growth Mindset is an absolutely essential tool for my toolbox. Does it take a place of prominence in your toolbox as well?

9. **Your Secret Weapon: Your Physical Health**. Success cannot buy you good health, but health can get you to success. This has everything to do with the energy, consistency, and vigor you get from good health—things no amount of success can buy. You can have a bold, powerful purpose and not be able to fulfill it because of poor health. If your current energy and health cannot sustain implementing what you need to do to fulfill your purpose, your well-crafted purpose may sit on a shelf collecting dust.

It is critical to take care of your body. Many people who suffer sustained mental lows have the same issue—they don't take care of themselves physically. How do you do this? Simple. You need to exercise (get off the couch and move in a meaningful way), get enough sleep on a consistent, daily basis (eight hours is ideal for most), and eat well to gain healthy energy. Taking energy supplements and drugging yourself with caffeine is not a substitute for sleep. Your mind will never be as sharp. You only have *one* body. Treat it well.

These are just a few of the mindset tools you need to have in your toolbox. They are your fundamental skills—your deep foundations—that you will continue to improve and hone over time. There are several other specific skill-set tools, depending on your purpose, that you will need as well.

Super Powers vary—from flying to telepathy, from speed to strength, from laser vision to super-hearing. Once you have your purpose, you have your Super Power. As you continue to live and flourish within your purpose, you will discover other areas for growth. You'll see which additional tools you need.

- If your purpose involves encouraging and inspiring others in some way or to some end, you will need to add several tools regarding interpersonal skills to your toolbox.

- If your purpose is to be a Godly parent, you will need to hone both your Bible knowledge and application, as well as your parenting skills.

- If your purpose is to work with young people to help them learn to be financially independent, you will need to tighten up your own finances—remember, teach by example and be a good mirror—and learn more about the financial challenges they face.

Once you have your purpose in mind, you need only give it some thought and you will find many other practical tools you need for your toolbox. Take a few minutes now and write down a few tools you might need. Then come up with the *first* step in getting each of those tools into your toolbox.

Don't overthink it. Just take the first step. Maybe that's signing up for a Bible study or calling a financially successful person you know who can give you insights. Perhaps it's pulling up and reading an article, calling a life or business coach, or simply seeking out someone whose purpose seems aligned with yours.

Carrying around an empty toolbox thinking that you can accomplish anything with it is, frankly, stupid—so just get started filling it with what you need!

As William H. Danforth says repeatedly in his book, *I Dare You!*, "Our most valuable possessions are those which can be shared without lessening; those which, when shared, multiply. Our least valuable possessions are those which when divided diminish."

This is a good way to look at your toolbox. Can you develop this skill to benefit both you and others? Will you be better because you shared it? These are your most valuable possessions.

"In simple terms, when you teach something effectively to somebody else, you are effectively learning it at a much deeper level" (Bartow and Selk, *Organize Tomorrow Today*). When you share your knowledge, you more deeply engrain it in your own mind. Help others and you help yourself as well. One of the people I coach sent this quote to me with a note alongside it that he now understands why I have been encouraging him to coach others while I coach him.

You are discovering valuable possessions—knowledge—which, when shared, multiply. It seems simple, yet people often have the opposite view. They believe that if they share their knowledge or possessions with others that they will have less. As Danforth said back in 1940, if that were true, those wouldn't be your most valuable possessions anyway.

22. Leap Tall Buildings

As we near the end of this book, it seems appropriate to leave you with a charge. You have a purpose, a power. It is your choice whether you make it a *Super* Power or not. Your Super Purpose will change and shape the lives and events around you. You have the ability to impact the world.

Be childlike in your aspirations, striving for what most adults would tell you is impossible. Others may think you waste your energies when you should conserve them. To continue the child analogy, it's a lot like gumballs. If you hoard gumballs, you merely have a pile of hard, uninteresting gumballs. They may be pretty to look at and show to your friends, but that is not their purpose.

Their purpose is to be used and enjoyed. When you use a gumball as it's meant to be used, you transform this hard ball of crunchiness into a soft, malleable, flavorful lump that can be shaped and formed to create fun and excitement. You can blow bubbles with it!

Your purpose is like that, too. If you keep it in its pristine condition, never using and deploying it as it were intended, it will not do any good—you will have wasted your purpose. That is why your purpose is to be continuously shaped, expanded, and tested. Use it for your benefit and joy, and for others' too. Unlike bubble gum, your purpose won't go stale.

Your purpose may change. You may choose to deploy it in a new way. That's okay. You make that choice with intentionality and an understanding that it is your latest path, your newest purpose, your mission.

Are you the type of person who will simply hoard your purpose, your talents, and the excitement, looking at it admiringly and even showing it off to your friends?

Or are you the kind of person who will fully develop and utilize your gifts, making the most of what's in your toolbox, in order to truly live and fulfill your purpose, blowing ever-larger bubbles for the benefit of others and therefore yourself?

This choice is powerful and the key to feeling fulfilled. Think of your favorite Superhero. How good would their story be if they never used those powers to do good things for the world? What if the speedster never ran? the teleporter never went anywhere? the mind reader lived in total isolation? the strong man refused to lift more than a gallon of milk?

They would have a hole in them, a place very unfulfilled. They would know they had wasted their potential. You will feel no different if you fail to pursue your purpose in a powerful way.

There will be obstacles. You will encounter villains in the form of nay-sayers and others who may laugh and scoff at you. Pay little if any attention to small-minded people. Focus on your purpose and continue to develop the tools you need to reach the next level.

Put a plan in place to ensure that you won't fall back into old ways. You need accountability—both internal and external, vertical and horizontal—so that you have the ability to continue to build that bridge across the Grand Canyon to where you know you will be, aligned perfectly with your purpose.

In Part 2, we ended with a discussion of skyscrapers; in Part 3, the Grand Canyon. You've completed the exercises throughout this book. You know your purpose. You know how to make it a Super Purpose. I have only one final question . . .

What will your skyscraper look like?

I can't wait to see it!

Conclusion

Congratulations and welcome to the ranks of the Supers! You are now equipped to live your life and pursue your purpose to the fullest. What makes you Super? You do.

- You have developed *Autonomy* through the powers of choice and intentionality and determined your own moral compass. You know who you are and define your own purpose and identity, refusing to let others do that for you. Having your own moral compass firmly intact allows you to avoid the effects of the changing norms of society.

  You stand as firmly as a rock. And, at the same time, you have the power to show empathy and compassion for other people.

- Your purpose—now a Super Purpose—guides you in the decisions you make and the actions you take. You are no longer swept from one unfulfilling activity to another. Your actions, activities, and attitudes have purpose. You have clarity. Goals are aligned with your ultimate purpose, and they are your goals, not someone else's.

You wake up each day energized and go to sleep each night fulfilled in moving your purpose forward.

Your skyscraper is starting to take shape as the foundations go deep and wide and the floors begin to rise above ground, building your legacy. You are the architect of this majestic building, which represents your purpose.

- Mastering your own issues, both internal and external, has allowed you to take your purpose and transform it into a *Super* Purpose. And you into a Superhero. You recognize your villains and Super-villains, your Kryptonite and your energy leeches. You are prepared to defeat them. Like the waters that formed the Grand Canyon, you are prepared for adversity. You welcome it.

- You are prepared to connect with other Superheroes who are driven with passion to pursue their purposes. They boost your energy, just as you boost theirs. Your toolbox awaits you. How will you choose to fill it? It's an exciting, invigorating journey. It's a breath of fresh air to finally know your direction—your purpose—and how to get moving.

Do you recall the analogy of the butterfly and the moth? You are about to burst from your cocoon. It's time to fly.

You've chosen your Super Power—now . . . go Live With Purpose, On Purpose, and Rock Your Super Self!

Mindset Toolbox

Contingency Mindset: The Contingency Mindset involves finding ways around obstacles that arise. People with this mindset are often viewed as opportunists. It is fundamental to being a strategist. Using if-then statements can help people rewire their brains to see paths around obstacles.

Experimenter's Mindset: An experimenter, like a scientist, follows the scientific method to test hypotheses. An experimenter does not physically or emotionally suffer if the test doesn't work as they had planned. They realize they've merely found one way that does not work along the path to finding what does work.

Obstacle Mindset: People who view most of what happens in the world around them as negative have an Obstacle Mindset. They tend to operate more on raw emotion than rational thought. They are the herd. This mindset can be either internal (negative self-talk) or external ("The world is falling apart around me. Why bother trying!").

Opportunity Mindset: People who see opportunity where others see an obstacle have an Opportunity Mindset. They tend to be happier, more positive people. This mindset can be either internal (focus on personal growth and development) or external (doing the opposite of the herd).

Strategic Mindset: People with a Strategic Mindset have the ability to see well beyond current obstacles and find opportunities to further their purpose. They anticipate other obstacles that may arise and plan around them. They keep the long-term vision and purpose in mind as they accomplish short-term objectives.

Growth Mindset: The Growth Mindset is the culmination of several of the other mindsets. To be able to have a Growth Mindset, you must have:

- An Experimenter's Mindset where you are searching for constant improvement.

- An Opportunity Mindset to keep focused on finding opportunities in every situation.

- A Contingency Mindset to have the tools necessary to proactively move past obstacles.

- A Strategic Mindset to be able to think well past any current obstacles and maintain long-term vision while accomplishing shorter-term objectives.

Resources

Introduction:
www.bgco.org/wp-content/uploads/2010/11/DEVELOPING-A-PURPOSE-STATEMENT.pdf

Chapter 2:
S&P 500 and investor returns over the 20-year period ending December 31, 2015 as cited by J.P. Morgan Asset Management and Dalbar's *Guide to the Markets—US.*

Chapter 6:
Covey, Stephen R., *Seven Habits of Highly Effective People* (Simon and Schuster, originally published in 1990)

Chapter 7:
Mumford, George, *The Mindful Athlete* (Parallax Press, 2015)

Chapter 9:
Goins, Jeff, *The Art of Work* (Nashville, Nelson Books, 2015)

Chapter 11:
Michael Bernoff: As founder and president of the Human Communications Institute, Michael has helped thousands of people transform their lives through his signature events, audio seminars and one-on-one coaching. Learn more at www.michaelbernoff.com

Claire Shipman, co-author of *The Confidence Code*, speech and Q&A on stage at a Women's Networking Conference, February 2016.

Brian Johnson, *Optimal Living 101* (see Chapter 17 notes)

Chapter 12:
Tracy, Brian, *Eat That Frog!* (Berrett-Koehler Publishers, 2nd Edition 2007)

Chapter 14:
Kay, Katty and Claire Shipman, *The Confidence Code* (HarperBusiness, 2014)

Claire Shipman, co-author of *The Confidence Code*, speech and Q&A on stage at a Women's Networking Conference, February 2016.

Collins, Jim, *Good to Great* (HarperBusiness, 2001)

Chapter 16:
Cardone, Grant, *The 10X Rule* (New Jersey, John Wiley and Sons, 2011)

Chapter 17:

Brian Johnson, creator of the *Optimal Living* website and movement to help people to "optimalize and actualize". Brian creates Philosopher's Notes TV, Master Classes, and much more. These are offered through his website www.brianjohnson.me.

> Note: Brian and his work have been a huge inspiration during the writing of this book. His insights, clarity in articulating complex concepts, and ability to cross-apply knowledge and teachings is a true gift. This is his Super Power, his Super Purpose.

Elrod, Hal, *The Miracle Morning* (Hal Elrod, 2012)

Carnegie, Dale, *How to Win Friends and Influence People* (Simon and Schuster, originally published in 1937)

Chapter 18:

Michael Bernoff, see Chapter 11 notes.

Selk, Jason and Bartow, Tom, *Organize Tomorrow Today* (Da Capo Lifelong Books, 2015)

Keller, Gary and Papasan, Jay, *The ONE Thing* (Bard Press, 2013)

Merriam-Webster Dictionary (2016)

Chapter 21:

Danforth, William H., *I Dare You* (St. Louis, "Privately printed", 1948)

Michael Bernoff , see Chapter 11 notes.

Selk, Jason and Bartow, Tom, *Organize Tomorrow Today* (Da Capo Lifelong Books, 2015)

Acknowledgements

I would like to acknowledge the countless people who helped to make this book, and my life, what it is. I was blessed from birth with amazing parents who obviously loved and cherished us. I think my mom always knew I was a little different than the other kids. She, along with my hard-working dad, taught me many lessons over the years which are integrated into this book. I wouldn't be who I am without them, and this book wouldn't be possible without them either.

My husband, Jeremiah, who tolerates my crazy ideas and is always ready to embark on a new adventure with me, has been a rock throughout the process. He works many hours to live his Super Purpose every day and gets few pats on the back for the immense, immeasurable work he does and the impact he has on the lives of his students. I have seen him transform children and adults in a short period of time. People who others thought were a lost cause, teaching them valuable life lessons while they learn the basics of martial arts. He is my superhero.

This list would not be complete without mentioning my children. It is for them that I write this as a part of my legacy to them and to the world. They are young now, only 8 and 2 years old. Our son is a brilliant, kind young man with a heart for others. Our little girl has a brilliant smile and infectious giggle. They are both much smarter than I am, and they light up my life. I look forward to watching them grow to be amazing people and hope to watch them define, develop and deploy their own Life Purposes . . . to become Supers.

Finally, to my editor (Spencer Borup), my coach (RE Vance), my early proof readers (Michelle Jarvis and Lia Wainwright), my long-time sidekick and friend (Becky Moseler) and the team of people who have chosen to become part of beginning of this movement toward Super Purpose, I say . . .

Thank you. Without you, this book wouldn't have a chance.

The team at Chandler Bolt's Self-Publishing School have been a wonderful and encouraging resource. Without the resources and direction they provided, I would likely have become lost in a sea of questions. Many kudos to the clear path they outlined which allowed me to reach this point at least a year before I had expected.

No successful journey to purpose happens in a vacuum. I am grateful to so many who have helped me in large ways and small, all of which are important.

Have a Super day!

About the Author

D.C. Hackerott

D.C. Hackerott was often referred to, in her much younger days, as Wonder Woman. Apparently, a few people thought she looked like the super hero. Feeling compelled to live up to this moniker, she is now the mother of two young children whom she loves, and is married to her husband who occasionally dresses as Batman.

By day, she has been a financial advisor for 17 years and wakes up--way too early--to be able to write books before the kids want breakfast. She occasionally escapes dirty diapers, dishes and laundry by helping teach, train, and coach other budding superheroes in the financial industry – far from home.

By night, DC and her husband, Jeremiah, own a martial arts school where they teach taekwondo and jiu-jitsu (with kids underfoot). They are both 6th degree black belts in taekwondo and are great friends to have in a dark alley.

In her ample spare time, she dirt bikes, camps, shoots, travels, and is an avid reader. Her motto is "The devil lives in your comfort zone. He likes it when you live there with him . . . so GET OUT!"

In her "former" life, she taught at Kansas State University in Economics and Finance for nearly six years, was a television anchor-woman and radio disc jockey during college, and married her amazing husband in a skydive wedding in 2002. She currently serves on several charitable and advisory boards as well as serving as a business and life coach and trainer.

Made in the USA
Columbia, SC
05 May 2019